BASICS
for Belief

BASICS
for Belief
Second Edition

Joseph D. Allison, Editor

Warner Press
Anderson, Indiana

Coordinator of Publishing & Creative Services
Church of God Ministries, Inc.
PO Box 2420
Anderson, IN 46018-2420
800-848-2464
www.chog.org

To purchase additional copies of this book, to inquire about distribution, and for all other sales-related matters, please contact:

 Warner Press, Inc.
PO Box 2499
Anderson, IN 46018-2499
800-741-7721
www.warnerpress.org

Cover and text design by Carolyn Frost
Copyediting by Stephen R. Lewis

ISBN-13: 978-1-59317-318-0

Printed in the United States of America.

08 09 10 11 12 13 14 /VP/ 10 9 8 7 6 5 4 3 2 1

CONTENTS

PREFACE
to the Second Edition

I n 1974, the Publication Board of the Church of God issued the first edition of this book for mass distribution, subsidized by the church's literature evangelism budget. Tens of thousands of copies were given to visitors and newcomers at local Church of God congregations. *Basics for Belief* was an excellent introduction to the beliefs of the movement, especially for those who came from other Christian backgrounds.

The eight contributors were Church of God pastors and evangelists. All of them were frequent contributors to our national periodicals, so they knew how to explain complex theological ideas in a way that laypersons could understand. They were ideally suited to this assignment. Most of these writers are now deceased, so their names may not be familiar to current readers. Allow us to introduce them briefly:

Adam W. Miller (d. 2003) served as a missionary to Japan (1922–27), secretary of the Missionary Board of the Church of God (1933–46), and second dean of the Anderson School of Theology (1953–62). His books include *A Brief Introduction to the New Testament* (1943) and *A Brief Introduction to the Old Testament* (1964).

Rolla O. Swisher (d. 2005) was a pastor and evangelist in California and Arizona and a longtime member of the Publication Board. A frequent contributor to the church's national periodicals (*Gospel Trumpet, Vital Christianity,* and *Pathways to God*), Pastor Swisher also wrote three books, including *When You Lead Devotions* (1961).

Hillery C. Rice (d. 2001) held long, successful pastorates in West Virginia and Indiana. He served on the Warner Press Board of Directors (1958–70). His book publications included *Tell Me about the Church* (1956) and *God's Happy People* (1965).

Milburn H. Miller (d. 1998) served as a pastor in Ohio and Indiana, and was a frequent writer for Church of God periodicals and adult curriculum materials. His book publications included *Ideas for Sermons and Talks* (1957) and *Notes and Quotes for Church Speakers* (1960).

Gene W. Newberry has been a prolific writer and teacher for all of his adult life and served as the third dean of Anderson School of Theology (1962–74). He was a longtime columnist for *Vital Christianity* and author of several books, including *A Primer for Young Christians* (1955). Now living in Anderson, Indiana, he self-published his autobiography, *A Boy from Lewis County*, in 2000.

Dewayne B. Bell (d. 1988) had a distinguished career as a college professor and pastor in Southern California. He served for several terms on the Publication Board, from 1953 until the mid-1980s, and frequently wrote for *Vital Christianity*.

Kenneth E. Jones (d. 1999) taught and served as dean at Gulf-Coast Bible College in Houston, Texas, which later moved to Oklahoma City, Oklahoma. (This institution is now known as Mid-America Christian University.) Dr. Jones's books included *Divorce and Remarriage in the Bible* (1989) and *A Theology of Holiness and Love* (1995).

W. Dale Oldham (d. 1984) was a popular evangelist who served as pastor of several congregations in Ohio and Indiana. He was the first regular speaker for the *Christian Brotherhood Hour* radio broadcast, and he served as president of the Publication Board (1948–58). His book publications included *Living Close to God* (1957) and *How to Grow Spiritually* (1968).

This second edition has updated historical references and clarified some terms for twenty-first-century readers. We have used the New Revised Standard Version for most Scripture quotations, rather than the New English Bible, which is seldom available to today's readers. Editor's notes highlight how Church of God beliefs compare to those of other Christian groups. We have also published a separate study guide to help you delve into some of these issues more thoroughly.

We trust that these changes will make *Basics for Belief* as useful to this generation as the first edition was to another. May it introduce newcomers to the movement in a thought-provoking way and stimulate dialogue between Church of God people and their friends.

INTRODUCTION
Welcome to the Conversation

While attending a conference some twenty years ago, I fell into a conversation with Donald W. Dayton, of Northern Baptist Theological Seminary. Dr. Dayton is a leading authority on the Wesleyan Holiness movement, so when I mentioned my Church of God connection, his eyes lit up. As I recall, our conversation went something like this:

"You're with the Church of God!" he exclaimed. "My, you have a rich heritage, don't you?" He cited the important role that D. S. Warner and other Church of God pioneers played in the Holiness Revival. He commented that the Church of God is one of the largest groups in the Wesleyan Holiness movement. (In point of fact, we're now the second largest, after the Church of the Nazarene.)

"You're Anabaptist, too, aren't you?" he said. "Not all Wesleyan churches are." Our Anabaptist background means that we not only practice believers' baptism ("So you're part of the Believers' Church."), but we also do other Anabaptist things: We keep the ordinance of foot washing, encourage modesty of dress, support conscientious objectors, and so on.

"You don't have bishops or district superintendents, like other Wesleyan and Anabaptist churches do," he continued. "Your congregational form of church government makes you somewhat like the Baptists. But they don't ordain women to ministry, and you do." He talked at some length about our congregational polity. He was curious to learn whether our General Assembly is similar to the Baptist national "conventions."

"You're also part of the Restorationist Movement," he said. Noting my puzzled expression, he explained that our vision for restoring the New Testament church is one that we share with the

Christian Churches, the Churches of Christ, and other groups that appeared in America about fifty years before the Church of God movement.

Then Dr. Dayton paused. "Why hasn't the Church of God taken more of a leadership role in the ecumenical movement?" he asked. "Your emphasis on Christian unity should put you at the forefront of that effort. Maybe you have some fundamentalist influences in your background as well."

I explained that Church of God people have always been actively involved in ecumenical work. (In recent years, for example, Gilbert W. Stafford, Edward L. Foggs, and Barry L. Callen have held leadership positions in national interchurch organizations.) However, we avoid formal ties with other denominations because our pioneers condemned the apostasy of those groups. I admitted that might seem like a fundamentalist attitude, but we have important differences with fundamentalists.

For example, we hold a high regard for the authority of Scripture, but we do not teach verbal inerrancy. We emphasize the importance of evangelism and missions, but we don't believe they will usher in a millennial reign of Christ. We read Bible prophecy as spiritual metaphor rather than geopolitical prediction, so we are amillennialists.

"Interesting!" Dr. Dayton said. "You're amillennialists. I didn't know that."

The next conference session was ready to begin, so we had to go our separate ways. As we shook hands, he said again, "So you're with the Church of God! Fascinating! I really need to learn more about you."

However, it seemed he already knew a good deal about us. Dr. Dayton saw the Church of God as a busy intersection where many different forms of Christianity come together. That's even truer today. Most people worshiping in a Church of God congregation did not grow up in the movement. Some come as unbelievers, drawn to the gospel of Christ for the first time. More people come as

Baptists, Methodists, Lutherans, Episcopalians, Catholics, or some other brand of Christian—and they find a spiritual home in the Church of God movement.

While the Church of God is inclusive of all Christians, we do not tell everyone to "do as you please." Neither do we encourage our leaders to "teach as you please." We do not assume that all beliefs are equally valid, nor do we practice syncretism (attempting to forge many different—even contradictory—beliefs into a great amalgam of doctrine). Instead, when other people share their beliefs with us, we "examine the Scriptures" to see whether they are true (cf. Acts 17:11). Careful Bible study and discussion are a vital part of our church life.

This book recognizes that fact. It identifies beliefs that Church of God people have in common with other Christians and shows how our beliefs and practices differ from those of other groups. The compare-and-contrast method was an important feature of the book when it was first published in 1974, and we have inserted editor's notes to make it even clearer. We have also prepared a study guide to help you dialogue with Christians from other traditions. After all, you will find several of them in your own congregation!

Don Dayton was right: We have a rich heritage, and we are a "fascinating" people. God is using us in a unique way to extend his kingdom, because we welcome all kinds of Christians into our fellowship and we're eager to learn from one another.

No matter who you are or where you came from, if you are a Christian, you are part of the Church of God. So pull up a chair and join the conversation.

Joseph D. Allison
Anderson, Indiana

CHRISTIAN UNITY

Adam W. Miller

There is a gathering tide of interest among Christians around the world to realize the unity for which Christ prayed. This interest in Christian unity has been called "the great new fact of our era."[1] As never before, Christians face the fact that the church, the body of Christ, has been torn asunder. We realize the wrongness and sinfulness of such division.

Through the centuries, the differences and the schisms have mounted, beginning with the Eastern Orthodox and Roman Catholic churches breaking apart; and since the Protestant Reformation in the sixteenth century, divisions have multiplied. Both Protestant and Orthodox Christianity have divided and subdivided, creating such confusion that only experts can now trace the lines of division. In the United States, there are more than two hundred separate Protestant communions, of which nearly eighty have more than fifty thousand members each.[2]

A divided church confuses our witness when we go to the mission field. New Christians in Asia and Africa are bewildered by the divisions of the churches in America and Europe. A church divided in spirit is a church unfaithful to its Lord, who clearly prayed that all of his followers should be one. To talk of the love of Christ is blasphemy unless we love all of his followers. To talk of the Christian love of neighbor is a mockery in the ears of the world unless we demonstrate it in our own household of faith. How can the church be the "bride of Christ" (Eph 5:25–27) if she is many brides? How can it be a "gathered flock" (John 10:16) if it is scattered? How can

---

1. William Temple, *The Church Looks Forward* (London: Macmillan, 1944), 4.

2. Eileen W. Lindner, ed., *Yearbook of American and Canadian Churches 2006* (Nashville, TN: Abingdon Press, 2006), viii, 373–85.

it be the body of Christ (Rom 12:5; 1 Cor 12:27) if it is broken and sacrificed by hands other than his own? In simple faithfulness to Jesus Christ our Lord, we must seek to heal the dividedness of the church and create an atmosphere within which all Christians may find their real unity in Christ.

The Intention of Jesus

The intention of Jesus with regard to the unity of the church and the oneness of his disciples is well stated in John 17. That chapter is a prayer, and it is with the deepest respect and reverence that one enters into a study of it.

It is a memorable prayer. Read it over again, especially verses 11 and 20–23. Christ wanted all Christians to be one. Verse 23 suggests that the unity of Christians ought to be as close and as real as that between Christ and the Father in heaven. A study of this prayer shows that the unity of the church is to correspond to the mutual indwelling of the Father and the Son. Such unity was to have its basis in each individual's having an inner connection with every other Christian. Such a union is close indeed, so close as to be indivisible: Christ dwelling in his disciples and the Father dwelling in both, so that the union is perfected. These are high levels of spiritual experience. This is what filled the mind and heart of Christ in his last hours. We are sure that the oneness he prayed for represents something far beyond that which Christians have yet realized. Christian unity is not a small and insignificant thing; it is a lofty spiritual realization, experienced only in the realm of the deepest fellowship with God and Jesus Christ. Such indeed was the intention of Jesus. It was precisely this kind of unity that would convince and impress the world.

Paul's Understanding of Christian Unity

In Ephesians 4:1–6 and 5:25–27, we have Paul's vision of the ideal church. Here the church is the bride of Christ, which Christ loved and for which he gave himself, that he might sanctify it, having made "her holy by cleansing her with the washing of water by the word, so as to present the church to himself in splendor, without a spot or wrinkle or anything of the kind...so that she may be holy and without blemish" (5:26–27). In the inspired imagination of the apostle, this church is almost personal in its unity. All of its members come together as a full-grown person, "to the measure of the full stature of Christ" (4:13). It is Christ's body, the fullness of him, that fills all in all. It is in and through the church that the manifold wisdom of God is revealed. It is the end of all God's works; creation and redemption are consummated in it. When the church is presented to Christ, as the bride to the bridegroom, the goal of history will have been reached. The apostle sees no more, but he ascribes glory to God, in the church, in Christ Jesus, through all ages, world without end (Eph 3:21). Such a vision of the church, unified and sanctified, arouses within us a sense of total commitment to work and labor that the dividedness of the church may be healed and this glorious ideal realized.

What does Paul mean when he speaks of "the unity of the Spirit" (Eph 4:3)? When some speak of the unity of the Spirit, they seem to have in mind a rather vague agreement that cannot be represented in real life. Certainly this is not the New Testament meaning, for the unity of the church is a unity of the Spirit. The church is one because it all of its members are animated by the same Spirit—the Holy Spirit.

This phrase conveys something of the tremendous significance of Paul's conception of unity. Because Christian unity is a spiritual reality, the following are true:

- Christian unity is not to be realized merely by maintaining uniform practice.

- Christian unity cannot be enforced by compulsion.

- Christian unity cannot fail to produce agreement among Christians on vital issues of faith.

- Christian unity must be expressed in outward unity.

- Christian unity confirms that we live under the lordship of Christ.

We may have outward unity that does not express inward unity. But if there is true inward spiritual unity, it will inevitably express itself in outward unity. A supposed inward unity that does not express itself outwardly is a negation of unity. So when Paul declares there is "one body, and one Spirit," he affirms a unity of the Spirit perfectly corresponding to the unity of the body.

Some Christians would dismiss the discussion of Christian unity, assuming that it is merely a theological or an ecclesiastical question and does not affect the work of evangelism and the promulgation of the gospel. Certainly this is not true. Paul contended that the one life of Christ was to be manifested in the *one body*. If the New Testament teaches anything at all, it teaches this.

Paul was an ambassador to the Gentiles. Before he started on his mission, he took the opportunity to go up to Jerusalem first to make the acquaintance of Peter. In this we see the great apostle beginning his lifework with an act of unity. Even though Paul had been called of God and had been given the great commission of an apostle, he thought it necessary to obtain the recognition of his Christian brethren. Here we see a policy of unity that dominated the whole lifework of Paul.

After fourteen years of labor for Christ, during which time he met with marked success in establishing churches, he still felt a great anxiety. What if he had run in vain? He feared that after having reached the goal he might be disqualified. Why? Certainly he had demonstrated his ability to win converts and establish churches among the Gentiles, yet he met with the Council of Jerusalem (Gal 2:1–10). Paul did not want to bring into existence a Gentile church or, worse, a Gentile denomination. Paul felt that he would have failed if he had not brought his Gentile converts into the *one fellowship*, the *one body*, the *visible church of God*.

The early church depicted in the pages of the New Testament expressed unity as *koinonia*. For centuries, Bible students have been trying to catch the full meaning of the state of the early Christians through an understanding of this Greek term. The most usual translation has been that of "fellowship," but the varied usage of that term has tended to weaken the meaning and confuse the understanding of the true spiritual state and condition of the church. The qualities of *koinonia* made the difference between a motley Jewish sect and a church with an evangelistic fire that flamed across continents as a world religion. What were those qualities?

The *koinonia* passage is found in Acts 2:42ff. This passage describes three basic conditions of that early church, and these throw light upon the true meaning of *koinonia*. These conditions were *commitment*, *corporateness*, and *responsibility*.

The early Christians were devoted to the apostles' teaching and fellowship; as a body of Christians, they spent much time together and they had all things common. Here was commitment and unity. They were responsible to and for each other, responsible to worship and act and live in the tenets of the faith to which they had been converted, and responsible to broadcast the gospel of Jesus Christ. The Christians were corporately responsible for the redemption of the world. For them, the redemptive mission of the church was an affair of the whole church. They were corporately responsible for the whole gospel. Their commitment to that responsibility made it possible for the warm breath of the love of God to blow on the sails of the ship of the church so that it sailed triumphantly through the centuries and into the lives of generation after generation of mankind. Here was togetherness. Their unity expressed itself in each one's being responsible to and for each other, and in corporately going forth to communicate the good news of salvation in Jesus Christ. This is the type of unity we need to find in our day, the *koinonia* we need to experience in each local church. This type of unity will send the gospel flaming across the world again.

The Degree of Unity Realized in the First Centuries

One cannot read the New Testament without noting that the early church had to battle the tendency toward division. Within the church at Corinth, for example, Paul had to remind the Christians severely that one Christian was not of Paul and another of Apollos, but that all were one in Christ (1 Cor 1:12–13). In spite of this early tendency toward division, one of the marvels of the first-century church was the degree to which Christians realized the ideal of unity. Living as we are, more than twenty centuries from that time, it is difficult for us to imagine what a strange picture the early church presented to that ancient world: "Masters and slaves sat side-by-side at the table of their common Lord as brethren beloved. Patrician ladies from the royal court and plebeian prostitutes from the public streets worshiped together as sisters saved. Roman freedmen, Greek philosophers, Jewish tradesmen, and Scythian barbarians met in the assembly upon such a plane of equality as the world had never deemed possible. People of all nations forgot their past and worshiped together in present unity of Spirit, purpose and life. Here was a marvel indeed."[3]

Lines of Advance toward Christian Unity

We have pointed out the dividedness of Christianity today and called attention to the rising tide of interest in healing that dividedness. Let us now consider some possible lines of advance toward this realization:

Recognition of the Nature of the Church. Our approach to Christian unity must begin with a recognition of the nature of the church as revealed in the New Testament, for an understanding of Christian unity is closely related to the meaning of the church. Wrong ideas of the church naturally lead to inadequate concepts of Christian unity. Any approach to Christian unity must distinguish between organized Christianity (which today is referred to as "the

---

3. Doremus A. Hayes, *The Heights of Christian Unity* (New York: Abingdon Press, 1927), 28.

church") and the true church as revealed in the New Testament. That church is composed of all those who are vitally united to Christ by virtue of their having received his salvation. So we should look carefully at the biblical meaning of the church.

Some people think the church is the sum total of all Christian groups. This is an erroneous concept if the true church is composed of those who have been brought into a personal relationship with Christ, because many members of organized churches have no vital relationship with Christ. Obviously, they are not really part of the church in the New Testament sense of that term. On the other hand, many believers stand outside of organized Christianity, seeking to make manifest to the world the life of Christ and give expression to the spiritual unity that fills such a large part in the writings of Paul.

Because of this complex situation, any biblically valid movement toward Christian unity must begin with a clear understanding of the real nature of the church. This we cannot emphasize too strongly.

To Witness to the Nature of the Unity We Seek. Christians must bear witness to this fact of the spiritual nature of the church as distinct from organized Christianity. Such a witness can be a contributing factor in the awakening of Christian men and women to the nature of the unity we seek—a practical unity through the Holy Spirit. Such a witness would prompt nothing less than a reformation within the church, a genuine renewal of the church.

Renewal and reformation must always be operative within the church; that has been an accepted principle of Protestantism. The kind of renewal clearly at work in the sixteenth century may work within the church today to translate into reality our hopes and longings for Christian unity.

Following the sixteenth-century reformation, the Methodist movement, Pietism, and kindred movements continued the work of renewal within the church. This places the work of D. S. Warner and his nineteenth-century associates within the same historical stream as they strived to advance the church in the direction of the ideal of Christian unity. So we are on solid historical ground as we seek to lift the witness of the New Testament concept of the church and the ideal of Christian unity.

"We Reach Our Hands in Fellowship." The words of an early Church of God hymn expressed a positive approach to Christian unity when it declared that "we reach our hands in fellowship to every blood-washed one." This means we must think of the church as a whole and not of one segment of it only. Since the church is those who have been brought into relationship with Christ through faith in his redemptive work, we must learn to think of the church in those terms. Christians not associated with us but possessing gifts of spiritual endowment belong to the whole body of Christ. Too often we are prone to think of them as holding a different relationship to God from that which we believe ourselves to hold. When we sing, "We reach our hands in fellowship to every blood-washed one," we draw the true circle of Christian unity that takes them in.

The Larger Vision. When Christians come to have a vision of the church as a whole, sectarian loyalties will be weakened and loyalty to the church entire will be strengthened. We need to give people a vision of the church universal that transcends anything that has ever been conceived by the human mind. Does the ordinary person realize that when he accepts Christ he is not merely becoming a member of a local congregation or of a group holding certain theological beliefs, but that he is being received into the fellowship of the most wonderful society the world has ever known? Does a university student who has caught the vision of global ministry find her outlook widened by the church, into whose fellowship she has come through the marvelous experience of salvation? I fear that our message has too often been weak at this point.

Group Movement in South India. In 1957, twenty congregations of Christians who had been known as the Bible Faith Christians came into contact with the Church of God movement in South

India. They began to sense that their own convictions paralleled those they heard taught in the Church of God. This led them to seek conversations with leaders of the Church of God movement in South India. Together the leaders of both groups studied the New Testament, and each recognized that the Holy Spirit was bringing them together in a relationship and experience of oneness they had never known before. This oneness resulted from the working of the Holy Spirit and their common understanding of the Word of God. There was nothing artificial about it at all. The sense of hunger for oneness with their Christian brothers found fulfillment under the dynamic workings of the Holy Spirit.

Cooperation with Other Christians. Denominational leaders often refer to cooperative unity. A growing spirit of cooperation is evident throughout the whole Christian movement. This spirit of cooperation is especially noted in Protestantism, where cooperative efforts have accomplished much for the good of the world and the furtherance of the missionary movement that otherwise would not have been possible. Dedicated men and women, bound together by the Holy Spirit, have been able to transcend denominational lines and work together for the common good of bringing salvation and other benefits of the gospel to multitudes of people in lands overseas.

We have one concern at this point. There seems to be a tendency on the part of many to accept this growing spirit of cooperation as a substitute for the unity for which Christ prayed and for which Paul labored with such dedication. This we must not do.

Cooperative efforts of dedicated Christians bring them closer to each other. Through their witnessing and sharing of ideals related to the nature of the church and of Christian unity, they can take a step closer to the New Testament ideal.

Work to Realize the Ideal in the Local Church. Perhaps nothing has weakened the witness of the church for Christian unity more than the lack of unity that often exists between local congregations. While we seek to heal the national and international divisions of

Christianity, we must also work to heal any dividedness in our local churches.

I know of no better way to do this than to make Christian experience deep and meaningful for our people. Too often the doctrines of salvation and entire sanctification are taught as mere theological concepts. But when people truly encounter God, their hearts are filled with amazement, wonder, and appreciation. We must never lose this sense of wonder at what God has done in our lives.

We must give content and meaning to the doctrines we teach. As we deepen the spiritual life of individuals in our local congregations, we will move toward effecting local unity. Our people must learn how to live in a group of people whose personalities are different and whose ways of doing things follow different patterns. Here is where the love of God, shed abroad in our hearts by the Holy Spirit, will enable us to triumph.

"One Lord, One Faith"

We have spoken of the unity of the Spirit and how that unity should express itself within the one body. An important aspect of that unity is the unity of the faith. Paul addresses this in Ephesians 4:11–13:

> The gifts he gave were that some would be apostles, some prophets, some evangelists, some pastors and teachers, to equip the saints for the work of ministry, for building up the body of Christ, until all of us come to the unity of the faith and of the knowledge of the Son of God, to maturity, to the measure of the full stature of Christ.

Note Paul's words: "until we all attain to the unity of the faith." He says that unity of faith must be attained through the ministry of pastors, teachers, evangelists, and others who have teaching and leadership gifts from the Holy Spirit.

The pioneers of the Church of God reformation movement sought renewal of the church around certain basic convictions. They were aware that the Christian movement in general had departed from these important teachings of the Word of God. As a movement, we use the name *Church of God* in an inclusive rather than in a denominational sense, for this is actually a movement toward Christian unity and the reestablishment of the New Testament standard of faith and life. We are striving to turn the tide in the direction of a recovery of the New Testament faith. We can only mention those basic convictions here, but the flowering of the Church of God movement has come from these beliefs:

- *Back to the Bible.* We make a deliberate effort to return to biblical revelation and to the authority of God's Word for our faith and practice.

- *Christian experience.* All of the doctrines of Christian experience—such as the new birth, entire sanctification, and the baptism of the Holy Spirit—are in reality descriptions of great experiences of the soul. Before they were ever formulated and expressed as doctrines, they were experienced.

- *The Church as the body of Christ.* Because Christians have lost sight of the true nature of the church, the renewal of the church depends upon a strong emphasis of this truth.

- *Christian unity.* This has been explained at some length already. Clearly, our Lord expects his church to be united here and now, not simply at the end of time.

The "one faith" of New Testament Christianity was not limited to these four things. However, the Church of God movement has expressed these four convictions with the following general doctrinal emphases:

1. *Belief in the divine inspiration of the Scriptures.* We affirm the authority and validity of the Scriptures for life today.

2. *Salvation through the atonement of Christ.* This doctrine of salvation includes the work of the Holy Spirit in convicting the sinner, effecting the work of regeneration, and producing the witness of the Spirit. Believers have the testimony of God that pardon and acceptance have taken place.

3. *Sanctification, or the experience of holiness.* The Holy Spirit accomplishes this work in the heart of a believer who has already realized salvation. This is why it is often referred to as the *second work of grace.* This fresh outpouring of the Holy Spirit in the heart of the already regenerate believer is the guarantee of personal sanctification and holiness.

4. *The church.* We believe God has clearly defined the true nature of the church in the New Testament, as already described in these pages.

5. *The ordinances of the church.* We believe baptism is by immersion and for believers only. Foot washing is practiced as an ordinance (i.e., a symbolic act for believers to perform because it is ordained by Christ). The Lord's Supper is also observed as a memorial and as an act of worship.

6. *Divine healing.* God promises to grant his people physical healing upon conditions laid down in his Word.

7. *The personal return of Christ.* We find no biblical evidence that his return will be connected with any millennial reign. The kingdom of God has already been established and is here and now, though its full realization is future and beyond history.

Future stages of development on the road to Christian unity may be hidden from us now. However, let us ask God for a deeper understanding of its meaning and give ourselves for its realization.

Let us never lose sight of the New Testament vision of the church. Concerned Christians today are expressing, more and more, their vision of what they hope and pray for.

SALVATION
Rolla O. Swisher

No loving mother could look more hopefully into the face of her firstborn than our heavenly Father looked into the cradle of the human race in the garden of Eden. God hoped that his children would share his passion for building the kingdom of God on earth.

> When I look at your heavens, the work of your fingers, the moon and the stars that you have established; what are human beings that you are mindful of them, mortals that you care for them? Yet you have made them a little lower than God, and crowned them with glory and honor…O Lord, our Sovereign, how majestic is your name in all the earth! (Ps 8:3–5, 9)

How are we different from animals? What is so special about human beings? A skeptic said, "Man is just an animal with the same fundamental urges and drives as the other animals. In fact, he is not much more than an educated ape."

"Very well," said one Christian scientist, "I will accept your reasoning when a cow pauses on a hilltop to contemplate the glory of the sunset or a dog stops as he bays at the moon to construct astronomical systems. Man does these things, and many, many more. I will consider the animals on a level with man when they do them too." A good answer!

The question raised in Psalm 8—"What are human beings?"—is answered in Genesis 1:27, "So God created humankind in his image." What does that mean? In what respects are we created in the image of God?

The Bible does not mean that we were created in the bodily form of God. Rather, we are made with some of the characteristics of God. God is holy—and human beings were created holy, without sin, and morally pure. But we were also created with the power of choice, which is a part of "the image of God." We are intelligent creatures. We are enough like our Creator to know right from wrong. We are able to discern, to judge, to know.

Being created in "the image of God" also means that we are made in the spiritual likeness of God. Human beings are more than physical matter, more than dust—we are, like God, spirits. We are made of tangible flesh and intangible spirit. We possess souls and bodies. It is incorrect to say that my body has a soul; rather, my soul has a body, since the real part of me will not go into the grave.

Jesus said, "Do not fear those who kill the body but cannot kill the soul; rather fear him who can destroy both soul and body in hell" (Matt 10:28). Even the Old Testament declared, "The dust returns to the earth as it was, and the breath returns to God who gave it" (Eccl 12:7). "And just as it is appointed for mortals to die once, and after that the judgment, so Christ, having been offered once to bear the sins of many, will appear a second time, not to deal with sin, but to save those who are eagerly waiting for him" (Heb 9:27–28). "Though our bodies are dying, our spirits are being renewed every day" (2 Cor 4:16 NLT).

If we are so much like God, what separates us from him? How are we not like God?

God never withheld any good thing from his children. God gave the first human beings permission to eat of every tree in the garden of Eden (literally, "the garden of delight")—except one! "And the Lord God commanded the man, 'You may freely eat of every tree of the garden; but of the tree of the knowledge of good and evil you shall not eat, for in the day that you eat of it you shall die'" (Gen 2:16–17).

Human beings are God's highest creation, yet we are not automatons that must follow the Almighty's will unthinkingly. We are given the power to make choices—to choose God's way as it is revealed to us, if we will but do so. Sadly, our earliest ancestors chose to go their own way. Not until the New Testament, when redemption is effected in the person of Jesus Christ, is the "tree of life" once more clearly within sight. And again, the choice is left to us.

God desires willing service, not forced service. It was a very dangerous thing for God to give us the power of choice, for we could choose the wrong things. And that is exactly what we do! But if he had not given us a free will, we would be just like his other creatures.

If you think you are just an animal—perhaps a little brighter and a little stronger than other animals, but still an animal—you will suppose that your conduct does not make much difference. What does it matter whether you are honest, kind, chaste, or generous? But if you are a spirit created by God to be holy as he is, which is what the Bible says you are, then how you conduct yourself makes a tremendous and eternal difference. Our conduct is directed by our beliefs. It makes a profound difference in our lives when we believe that God has created us to be like him.

God did not create us and then abandon us. Even when sin came into the world, God promised that he would provide a way of salvation for us. "For a child has been born for us, a son given to us; authority rests upon his shoulders; and he is named Wonderful Counselor, Mighty God, Everlasting Father, Prince of Peace" (Isa 9:6).

There is a way out of our fallenness! Not only were we made by a great Creator, but he has placed the utmost value upon us—even to the extent that his Son would die so that we might be saved. "For God so loved the world that he gave his only Son, so that everyone who believes in him may not perish but may have eternal life. Indeed, God did not send the Son into the world to condemn the world, but in order that the world might be saved through him" (John 3:16–17).

All Have Sinned

Some people deny that they need to be saved. They feel they are good people, who have never done anything that needs to be forgiven by God. But Scripture says that "all have sinned and fall short of the glory of God" (Rom 3:23). Who would argue with that? What human being radiates "the glory of God"? Jesus Christ did. He came to redeem us, to adopt us into God's family, and to change our hearts. When we give our lives to Christ, we are not the same old creatures parading under a new name. The spirit of Christ now lives within us. "So if anyone is in Christ, there is a new creation: everything old has passed away; see, everything has become new!" (2 Cor 5:17).

When we have Christ in our hearts, we have eternal life. "And this is the testimony: God gave us eternal life, and this life is in his Son. Whoever has the Son has life; whoever does not have the Son of God does not have life" (1 John 5:11–12).

This is why God spoke into existence all of creation except us. With his loving hands, God formed the first human beings and breathed life into them (Gen 1:20–31; 2:1–7). So we were made for eternal fellowship with God. "For you are all children of light and children of the day; we are not of the night or of darkness" (1 Thess 5:5). We are made to be God's people—first through creation and second through redemption.

Christianity stands forever opposed to any belief system that has a deterministic view of mankind! In a regime that denies any God in the universe, people have no inherent value. They are merely objects to be pushed around. But in society founded on faith in God the Creator, each of us has certain privileges and rights as a child of God.[1]

The plan of salvation is one of substitution. God substituted his own life in the person of his Son, Jesus Christ, paying the pen-

---

1. Editor's Note: Contrast this with the doctrine of predestination, which some Christians believe. Predestination teaches that God decides whether a person will be saved or condemned, even before birth. The Church of God and other groups believe that God offers salvation to everyone and that he gives everyone the freedom to choose whether to accept that offer.

alty for our sins. In the suffering of the cross, the Lord Jesus Christ paid the debt that we owed for our sin. That's how much God loves us.

Christ "bore our sins in his body on the cross so that, free from sins, we might live for righteousness" (1 Pet 2:24). Because Christ loved abundantly, he involved himself in our predicament. He became our substitute and bore the punishment for our sins. He went willingly to Calvary to provide a way of escape and new life for all who would accept the unlimited forgiveness of God.

The greatest love and forgiveness ever demonstrated on this earth were seen on that fateful day when Christ died for us upon the timbers of a Roman cross. His whole life was characterized by forgiveness. Again and again, he said to people whose lives were filled with evil, "Your sins are forgiven" (Luke 5:20; 7:48). He brought hope to the hopeless. He always had time to lift, to love, to forgive.

So our salvation is by atonement, not by attainment. The cross reveals both our sin and God's salvation from sin. Only in the presence of the cross can we know our sin; only in it can we see God and his saving grace.

What Must I Do to Be Saved?

The feet of first-century missionaries Paul and Silas were fastened in stocks in the Philippian jail. It was the midnight hour. They were singing and praying. An earthquake shook the old jail to its foundation. As the jailer came upon the scene, every door stood ajar. The jail was probably emptied now. The jailer was about to kill himself, because Roman law said that if a prisoner escaped, the jailer must suffer the penalty that the prisoner would have suffered. But just then, Paul "shouted in a loud voice, 'Do not harm yourself, for we are all here'" (Acts 16:28). In amazed relief, the jailer called for light and rushed into the presence of Paul and Silas to ask, "'Sirs, what must I do to be saved?' They answered, 'Believe on the Lord Jesus, and you will be saved, you and your household'" (vv. 30–31).

If we are living apart from God, spiritually lost and condemned, we too should ask, "What must I do to be saved?" And we should ask it before we drift so far that we cannot find our way back. We must repent, confessing that we are sinners and in need of Christ's saving power. We must forsake our sin and be willing to turn our backs upon it.

What sin? The sin that bars us from heaven is neglecting to accept Christ as our Savior and refusing to live for him. Jesus said, "Everyone therefore who acknowledges me before others, I also will acknowledge before my Father in heaven; but whoever denies me before others, I also will deny before my Father in heaven" (Matt 10:32–33).

When we pray for God's forgiveness, we must believe God answers our prayers. "If we confess our sins, he who is faithful and just will forgive us our sins and cleanse us from all unrighteousness" (1 John 1:9).

When we know Christ in the forgiveness of our sin, we experience a change of mind and a change of heart. Our entire reason for living is changed. Our ambitions and our affections all are recentered in the Lord Jesus Christ. We cannot do it by ourselves, but it can be accomplished by the help of God. Spiritual transformation is not merely a matter of keeping good resolutions, but of placing one's self utterly in the hands of Christ. Salvation brings us spiritual power, not only because it affects what we have done, but because it changes what we are.

One thing is clear: We cannot save ourselves. We must ask Christ to save us. However, there are some things we can do to make possible the working of God's saving power. We can establish a firm determination to live for the Lord. We can humble ourselves before the throne of God. We can believe that Christ is able, willing, and eager to redeem us.

We ought to throw up our hands and say, "Lord, I give up trying to run my own life. Won't you please take over?" If we will follow the pattern of repentance, confession, and faith—the pattern identified by the apostles and followed by the Philippian jailer—we will find full and satisfying salvation in and through the Lord Jesus Christ.

The Way to the Heart of God

Jesus invited twelve men to become his disciples by simply saying, "Follow me" (Matt 4:19). How strange the words must have sounded, coming from a carpenter of Nazareth! Yet the Twelve did follow him.

Christ's "Follow me" is the greatest and most important challenge given us. To follow Jesus requires more than obedience. It requires faith in his power. We must trust and obey! Following Christ is an enriching pilgrimage. It is the way to the heart of God. It is the only way to spiritual power.

A town in Washington state had grown up without the advantage of electricity. One day, the townspeople were told that a big dam was to be built across the river above them. When completed, it would furnish abundant power for their needs. So while the dam was being built, all of the houses in town were wired for electricity.

One evening the power was turned on unexpectedly, and in a home at the far end of the village the switches had been left on. Immediately, light flashed from every room. The homeowner rushed into the street and began shouting to his neighbors, "The power is on! The power is on!" Soon lights were streaming from every house in the neighborhood.

Something like that happens when you begin following the Lord Jesus Christ. He turns the power on, power for victorious living. So turn the power on! Make Christ the Savior and Lord in your life!

Salvation Makes You a Member of the Church

"And day by day the Lord added to their number those who were being saved" (Acts 2:47b). Our salvation experience in Jesus Christ makes us members of the church of the living God. To be in Christ is to be in the church!

After you have been converted, you need to follow the Lord in baptism. Baptism tells the church and the world that you are a Christian. Baptism does not save you. It is a symbol or picture of the deeper religious experience that was yours when you became a Christian. This is why the spiritual act of conversion must precede the symbolic act of baptism.[2]

A Christian is immersed in water to symbolize being dead to sin and buried. Then you are raised out of the water, testifying to the fact that you are not only dead to sin but vibrantly and gloriously alive to Jesus Christ, to righteousness, and God's way of life.

Of course, that is not the end of it. Salvation is just the beginning of your new life—a life that you will need to nurture every day. Prayer is one of the best ways to strengthen your spiritual life. Your soul craves for God, and his presence becomes known through prayer. Life can be one long prayer walk with the Lord as your companion. It was for Enoch (Gen 5:22–24).

Prayer demonstrates that in God "we live and move and have our being" (Acts 17:28). If you make the Lord your guide, "when you turn to the right or when you turn to the left, your ears shall hear a word behind you, saying, 'This is the way; walk in it'" (Isa 30:21).

Prayer, reading of the Bible, and meditation should be the daily habit of every Christian. Find the time, place, and method that will best fit into your daily devotional life.

Where should one begin devotional Bible reading? The gospel of John is a good place to start. This might be followed by reading Paul's Second Corinthian and Ephesian letters, then the epistles of

---

2. Editor's Note: Roman Catholics and some Protestants believe that baptism is a *sacrament*, i.e., it conveys spiritual merit or power. So they believe a person must be baptized in order to be saved. The Church of God and many other Protestant groups do not. We believe that baptism symbolically declares what God has already accomplished in a person's life; we do not believe that baptism has any saving power or conveys any spiritual merit.

Peter and John. From the Old Testament, the Psalms and Isaiah are inspiring and challenging.

Living the rich, abundant Christian life is not as effortless as sliding down hill in the snow. Every step forward requires purposeful determination to put the teachings and spirit of Christ in your daily talk, walk, and attitudes. God will enable you to do all of these things.

THE ORDINANCES
Hillery C. Rice

I n his sermon on the day of Pentecost, which gave birth to the New Testament church, the apostle Peter invited his hearers, "Repent, and be baptized every one of you in the name of Jesus Christ" (Acts 2:38). Thus, baptism is the completion of the penitent's experience.

Baptism is a ceremony of symbolic washing that signifies someone has accepted the Christian faith. Christian churches have used this ceremony since the days when Christ told his disciples, "Go therefore and make disciples of all nations, baptizing them in the name of the Father and of the Son and of the Holy Spirit, and teaching them to obey everything that I have commanded you. And remember, I am with you always, to the end of the age" (Matt 28:19–20).

However, the word *baptize* no longer has a clear meaning to many people. We have almost as many different modes of water baptism as we have varying religious groups. To one group, baptism is apparently essential to salvation. They believe those who are never baptized are doomed to perish. Another group absolutely ignores water baptism or any other church ordinance. This is perhaps due to revulsion to the sacramental aspect of baptism. Still others leave the question to the individual: "Let your conscience be your guide!" Biblically, baptism is commanded by Christ, and its observance is to continue "to the end of the age."

Multitudes of Christians among Protestant churches today have not been baptized. Perhaps the apathy toward this church ordinance is due largely to the vagueness and carelessness of the ministry. Sometimes the motivation for baptism emanates more from law than from love. Often a baptismal candidate is taken to an unsightly hole in the dark church basement or some other obscure location. The entire ordinance—from the location of the baptistery to the apparent secrecy of the occasion—so degrades a precious Bible truth that the candidate leaves the service in bewilderment and confusion.

Both pastors and laypersons need to rethink the significance of water baptism, for then and only then will it be cast in proper biblical context. In the midst of all the encouraging talk about Christian unity today, a Bible doctrine as vital as water baptism ought to be discussed openly. Paul, writing to the Ephesians (4:3–6), places baptism at the center of issues related to spiritual unity. To remove any of these issues from the discussion would be like taking away one section of the Golden Gate Bridge—you would have no bridge at all! To remove baptism from these seven emphases of Ephesians 4:3–6 is like cutting out the fourth link from a chain of seven.

Why Should I Be Baptized?

What symbolic act would better illustrate the death, burial, and resurrection of our Lord, and at the same time show how we also die to sin, bury the old life, and arise into a new life in Christ? Water baptism is the follower's visible badge of belonging to the Christian family. It is for believers only.

I have no right to wear the Kiwanis emblem on the lapel of my coat; neither am I permitted to display the pin worn by the Optimists, the Rotarians, members of the Civitan Club or the Exchange Club. It would be deceptive for me to wear any of these, for I have not conformed to the creeds and beliefs of these reputable groups. However, I have every privilege and right to wear the Lions emblem or display it in any manner that pleases me because I am a member of Lions International. I conform to the regulations and program of this particular service group.

Every born-again Christian has the right to Christian baptism; this is the believer's badge. Moreover, water baptism is enjoined upon every believer in love. Thus, Christian baptism is part and parcel of the Christian gospel.

Why should one be baptized? Paul, instructing the Roman church, wrote: "Do you not know that all of us who have been baptized into Christ Jesus were baptized into his death? Therefore we have been buried with him by baptism into death, so that, just as Christ was raised from the dead by the glory of the Father, so we too might walk in newness of life. For if we have been united with him in a death like his, we will certainly be united with him in a resurrection like his" (Rom 6:3–5).

Writing to the Galatian church, Paul had this to say: "As many of you as were baptized into Christ have clothed yourselves with Christ" (3:27). He means that in conversion an individual is immersed into Christ, dipped into and immersed into the Anointed One, the Messiah; and this truth is symbolized by water baptism. Baptism is our communication to others that there has been an outward washing that stands for an inward cleansing by the Spirit of Christ.

By no stretch of the imagination can one be saved by baptism. We are not Christian because we have been baptized. Rather, we are baptized in water because we have already been immersed in God's fountain of saving grace. Then, Christian baptism is a symbol of our membership in Christ and in his church.

In the above scripture, I find baptism to be a rite that publicly identifies every born-again Christian with the risen Savior. It is a bold testimony to other Christians and to the world. The ordinance of baptism is our witness that Jesus is the Christ, the Son of God, and that through faith we have life in his name. Thus, baptism is a dramatic proclamation of the gospel of Christ. It binds together a whole sheaf of truths:

Water baptism reminds us that we now belong to God; we are now engrafted as a branch on the living Vine. Christ's own experience at baptism seems to have confirmed his calling to go to the cross. So Christian baptism reminds us that we participate in the suffering, the death, the burial, the resurrection, and the new life of our Lord Jesus Christ. Thus, baptism motivates and influences our understanding of who we are as Christians. It is a way of walking, not merely a way of talking.

Why should someone be baptized? The follower of Christ often feels lonely. A believer reaches out for a closer tie with other Christians in order to experience the strength and undergirding of true Christian fellowship. The ordinances offer us a practical way to do this.

The Law of Moses was replete with rituals and symbolic ceremonies, all of which pointed forward prophetically to our redemption through Christ. Such ceremonies and ordinances were a common point of identity for members of the Jewish community. When the prophecies of redemption were fulfilled in Christ, such ceremonies no longer served any real purpose. It is, no doubt, to these outmoded ordinances that Paul refers in Ephesians 2:14–16 and Colossians 2:14. However, this does not mean that we cannot profit by keeping ordinances that do have current meaning for twenty-first-century Christians.

The entire plan of redemption centers in Christ, particularly his death and resurrection. This redemption does not merely alter our conduct. In reality it changes, from the heart, our entire outlook and attitude toward God and our neighbor. It seems, therefore, only fitting that Christian worship should incorporate concise and meaningful acts to symbolize such great spiritual truths. Christian baptism does this.

Baptism keeps our thinking properly focused on the person who saves us (Christ) and on the truths that are central to our redemption, spiritual growth, and maturity. As a human family is enlarged by the birth of more and more children, so is the family of God. Members are added to the church by the process that Jesus called being "born again." Water baptism is the convert's testimony to this spiritual birth.

The Power of Baptism

There is no mystical power in the ordinance of baptism, any more than in the ceremony of marriage. A wedding does not make a man and woman more husband and wife than they would be without the ceremony. However, the ceremony declares their intention and willingness to become one.

Baptism is not magic. Christ's command regarding baptism is a mandate; nevertheless, our Lord is wise, sensible, and practical. He realizes that circumstances sometimes hinder an individual from being baptized (e.g., the thief on the cross described in Luke 23:43). That does not prevent someone from being saved.

What minister has not been confronted with this problem: "Will you please baptize my brother? He is in a coma, and I am afraid he will die unsaved." To do so would squeeze the ordinance of baptism into a false theological mold. Water and words do not save one from eternal damnation. To baptize someone under such conditions publicly says that baptism is magic. "In Christ God was reconciling the world to himself" (2 Cor 5:19), not through water, but through Christ.

Baptism is a symbol of salvation. A symbol is an object or act that suggests a greater reality. To state this in a simple and understandable manner: Going down into the water signifies that a person's old life is dead and buried, that God has saved us "from sin," and that we have severed our relationship with sinful practices. Coming up out of the water signifies that we are resurrected to new life. We are new creatures in Christ Jesus (2 Cor 5:17).

When a Muslim is converted to Christianity, his family and friends dislike it, yet they deal with him kindly and seek to win him back. However, when he follows the Lord in baptism, they sever connections with him and drive him out from home and friends. To Muslims, water baptism holds a deep significance. They sense that baptism is a definite sign of conversion to Christ. They feel helpless to win a baptized Christian back to their camp.

Yet baptism is more than a symbol of conversion. When Peter preached, "Repent, and be baptized...and you will receive the gift of the Holy Spirit" (Acts 1:38), he indicated that baptism invites the Holy Spirit into our lives. At the baptism of Christ, the Holy Spirit appeared and the heavenly Father said, "This is my Son, the Beloved, with whom I am well pleased" (Matt 3:17).

What Is the Bible Method?

Another question often asked is, What is the true Bible method of water baptism? Our word *baptize* is an anglicized form of a New Testament Greek word. The Greek word is *baptizo*, which means "to dip in (or under) water." Immersion or dipping, then, is the biblical means of baptism. Christ observed this rite himself, for Scripture tells us, "He came up from the water" (Matt 3:16). Clearly, he had to go down into the water before he could rise out of it.

Bible scholars agree that immersion was the mode of the primitive church. Charles E. Brown made this point clear: "Even John Calvin, the great pioneer theologian of all the Presbyterian and Reformed churches in the world, said positively that immersion was the form of baptism in the ancient church. Here are his exact words: 'The very word *baptize*, however, signifies to immerse, and it is certain that immersion was the practice of the ancient church.'"[1]

There is abundant historical evidence that immersion was the mode used by the early church. Archaeologists such as Augusti, De Rossi, Garucci, Martigny, and De Vogue tell us that the remains of ancient baptisteries in Asia, Africa, and Europe prove conclusively that immersion was the accepted mode of baptism in the early days of the church. In Europe, some of these ancient baptisteries may still be seen. Both Eastern (Greek, Russian, Armenian, Nestorian, Coptic, and others) and Western churches practiced immersion and recognized nothing else for baptism.

1. Charles E. Brown, Editorial, *Gospel Trumpet*, December 2, 1950.

Who Should Be Baptized?

Who is a candidate for water baptism? Only born-again followers of Christ. This conviction is based upon both sound biblical exposition and careful interpretation of church history.

Two groups of people try to thwart God's plan of baptism. They are unredeemed people who insist on baptism and redeemed ones who reject baptism. Luke records: "But the Pharisees and experts in religious law rejected God's plan for them, for they had refused John's baptism" (Luke 7:30 NLT). On the other hand, Matthew tells us that when John the Baptist was baptizing in the Jordan, unrepentant people presented themselves to be baptized. Very frankly, he asked them, "You brood of snakes!...Who warned you to flee God's coming wrath? Prove by the way you live that you have repented of your sins and turned to God." (Matt 3:7–8 NLT).

Every born-again Christian is a candidate for this Bible experience. However, it ought to be pointed out that the Bible nowhere indicates that baptism is for infants. Remember that the church began its mission with this injunction: "Repent and be baptized." An infant cannot possibly repent, so the total concept of infant baptism is a human contrivance.

Over the years, a number of people have very conscientiously asked me about the church's stand on rebaptism. Is it biblical? Is there any reason why one should be baptized the second time? Any reason why a believer should not be rebaptized? Apparently, the ancient church, both Catholic and Protestant, did not repeat the ordinance of baptism. However, there is no New Testament scripture for or against such practice.[2]

A man I know was baptized as a boy, but later he completely fell away from a godly life, drifting into a worldly crowd and indulg-

---

2. Editor's Note: The Church of God is part of the Believer's Church tradition because we teach that baptism is only for people who believe and confess that Jesus Christ is their Savior and Lord. Since an infant cannot make such a decision, we do not practice infant baptism. For the same reason, we encourage people who were baptized as infants to be baptized again when they make a profession of faith as adults. This makes us part of the Anabaptist (literally, "baptizing again") tradition, along with the Mennonite, Brethren, and other church groups.

ing in sinful practices. He continued his life of sin for several years before returning to God. After he had been reclaimed, he asked to be rebaptized, and his request was granted. Now he has the clear conscience that comes from an up-to-date experience of salvation and baptism. By all means, Christians ought to make an authentic testimony of their relationship with God. If this means rebaptism, then do it!

When Should I Be Baptized?

Another pertinent question regarding baptism is, when should someone be baptized? The Bible is replete with examples of people being baptized immediately after conversion. We have no record of anyone waiting five, ten, or twenty years, or even thirty days, as far as that goes. It was a "now" experience with the first followers of Christ.

The penitent souls at Pentecost asked, "Brothers, what should we do?" Peter answered, "Repent, and be baptized every one of you." These eager, newborn souls leaped at the opportunity to obey, for the scripture says, "Those who welcomed his message were baptized" (Acts 2:41). The same immediacy is found in the men and women saved in Philip's revival in Samaria, in the Ethiopian eunuch, in the jail keeper at Philippi, and others.

In 1 John 5:3 we read: "Loving God means keeping his commandments, and his commandments are not burdensome" (NLT). Our Lord chided some people with the question, "Why do you call me 'Lord, Lord,' and do not do what I tell you?" (Luke 6:46). When we love someone, we are eager to please him, and the sooner the better. Isn't it rather strange that someone would make high claims of loving God and yet postpone baptism? Baptism is a public identification with Christ that brings added strength and victory to our lives. If you are a Christian but have not been baptized, do it now.

A word to my colleagues in ministry: We cannot rightly claim to preach the total gospel if we neglect the ordinance of water baptism. People being baptized are greatly blessed because they are obeying the command of Christ. Also, those who view this kind of service are influenced, challenged, and blessed. In recent years, I have planned baptism services as a central part of the morning worship hour. Sometimes baptism comes at the beginning of the worship hour; at other times, it is planned for the very center of the hour. At still other times, it is at the closing part of worship. But we always make it the central theme of the service and schedule it at a time when the most people are present.

Recently, we planned a baptismal service to be the very first part of the eleven o'clock worship hour. Just as the choir was seated, the curtains to the baptistery were opened and I began to baptize people. Many people who attended the service expressed their appreciation for our emphasizing this prime doctrine of the New Testament.

My sincere prayer is that more and more of our congregations will recognize the significance of water baptism, that baptism shall be made central in the worship and life of the church, and that everyone eligible for Christian baptism will avail themselves of the opportunity to follow the Lord Jesus in this observance. Water baptism is commanded by Christ Jesus, who is head of the church. If Christ tells us to do something, happy are we if we do it.

The Lord's Supper

Church of God congregations across the world today observe three ordinances. We have already considered water baptism. The second ordinance is Communion, or the Lord's Supper. Christian baptism is for born-again believers who desire to demonstrate the change in their lives through the power of Christ. Our continued dependence upon God is expressed through the experience at the Lord's Table, which adds profound meaning to the other ordinances.

From the very first year of the church's existence, Communion was observed by the followers of Christ. Here the sacred symbols are bread and wine, representing the broken body and the shed blood of our Lord's crucifixion. This can be traced directly to Jesus, who gathered the disciples in a last supper the night before he was put to death, giving them bread to eat and wine to drink.

What ritual could more appropriately commemorate the Lord's death and remind us that we are partakers of the divine benefits of the atonement than the Lord's Supper? In these solemn moments, we show that we are involved. We helped to shed his blood in the sense that our sins caused it; but in just as real a sense, we are recipients of the full benefits of atonement.

So long as we are physical beings, living on the earth, the only manner in which we shall see the spiritual is in material things. This is why Communion speaks to us. It is the outward and visible sign—the indication, the suggestion—of a spiritual, invisible grace. For those who recognize eternal values, a flag is more than a piece of bunting and a wedding ring is more than a circle of gold. So in the elements of Communion, we see the eternal truth of Jesus and sense his nearness.

Jesus said, "Do this in remembrance of me" (Luke 22:19). We are so prone to forget God and his kindness toward us that he gave us the Lord's Supper to remind us—at intervals that should not be too far apart—of his redemptive love for us, exemplified by Christ's suffering at Calvary.

Anyone who participates in this ordinance should prepare for it through self-examination. Who among us is without this need! The apostle Paul says, "Examine yourselves, and only then eat of the bread and drink of the cup" (1 Cor 11:28). The table sets the stage for the highest level of fellowship on earth. In this grand setting, we join heart, head, and hand with the redeemed around the earth. Every child of God ought to partake of the Lord's Supper as often as possible.[3]

---

3. Editor's Note: Church of God congregations practice open Communion, which means that all Christians are invited to partake.

The Lord's Supper reminds us that we have not given ourselves to a lost cause. It was instituted, says the apostle Paul, to "proclaim the Lord's death until he comes" (1 Cor 11:26).

Foot Washing

To conclude the three ordinances practiced by the Church of God, let me briefly discuss the ordinance of foot washing. Could we possibly invent a custom that would better illustrate our relationship to our Christian brothers and sisters? This rite was not designed to make us humble; we practice it to express our humble attitude toward other Christians. Unless there is pure love in our hearts toward others, we had better not practice it at all.

Men especially (even the best of them) tend to have feelings of unjustified pride and superiority. The practice of foot washing can greatly cultivate humility among a group of Christian men as we stand at a brother's side to acknowledge our love and esteem. Since human nature continues to "war against the Spirit," we need to repeat foot washing over and over to remind, cultivate, and sharpen our sensitivity to the Spirit of Christ.

Jesus said, "Whoever wants to be first must be last of all and servant of all" (Mark 9:35). Foot washing is a symbol of service, a badge of the humble servant. We must never forget that our Lord took a towel and conquered the world. The inspired writer reminds us that we should "love one another with mutual affection; outdo one another in showing honor" (Rom 12:10). And Christ gives the injunction, "If I, your Lord and Teacher, have washed your feet, you also ought to wash one another's feet. For I have set you an example, that you also should do as I have done to you" (John 13:14–15). Humility is so characteristic of the Christian that we ought regularly, systematically, and graphically to keep reminding ourselves of the spirit we share. Thousands of God's children find renewed spiritual strength in the observance of foot washing.[4]

---

4. Editor's Note: Other Christian groups that observe the ordinance of foot washing include Episcopalians, Mennonites, and the smaller Anabaptist denominations.

SANCTIFICATION
Milburn H. Miller

A friend once said to a prominent Christian writer, "What does the Holy Spirit mean to you?"

She replied, "Oh, one of the three persons of the Godhead—the third person of the Trinity."

"I sense something offhand in the way you say that," the friend said. "Let me guess: in your mind, the Spirit has an insignificant and unnecessary place. Isn't that right?"

The writer nodded, "That's right."

"I know from personal experience that the Holy Spirit is just as great, just as needed as the other two persons of the Trinity," the writer's friend explained. "Anyway, you still haven't answered my original question: What is he to you?"

She replied, "I've got to be truthful. He's nothing to me. I've had no contact with him and could get along quite well without him."

Here we see two viewpoints regarding the presence and purpose of the Holy Spirit that are so evident today. To many people, the Holy Spirit is a theological abstraction, a meaningless mystery. To others, he is real and indispensable. Which is he to you?

"Did you receive the Holy Spirit when you became believers?" the apostle Paul asked the Christians at Ephesus (Acts 19:2). The Ephesians said they knew nothing about the Holy Spirit. Paul then explained the necessity for each Christian to receive the Holy Spirit. They gladly heard his message and believed. The Holy Spirit came upon them. They immediately became transformed Christians. "So the word of the Lord grew mightily and prevailed" (19:20).

Perhaps you, like the Ephesians, have an insufficient understanding about the nature and work of the Holy Spirit. May the following pages help you to comprehend him better and surrender your life to him in a greater measure.

The Holy Spirit's work is beyond question a biblical doctrine. Any person honestly studying the Scriptures will conclude that the Holy Spirit is provided for every Christian. Yet some people rule out the significance of the coming of the Spirit into the life of the believer and his consequent work. God's plans for his children are good plans. We cannot improve upon them, nor should we try to eliminate any of them.

Many, many times in the New Testament, we find the words *Holy Spirit, Holy Ghost, the Spirit,* and *the Spirit of God.* There are frequent references to the Spirit in the Old Testament as well. The Holy Spirit has always had a definite place in the plans of God.

The life of the Christian is incomplete without the infilling, indwelling, and empowering presence of the Holy Spirit. The operation of the Holy Spirit is vital to the life and progress of the church, as well as to the success and victory of individual Christians. He lifted the disciples of Christ from a state of nominal spiritual health to a position of spiritual stability and effective service. He does the same for Christ's followers today.

The apostle Paul wrote, "Anyone who does not have the Spirit of Christ does not belong to him" (Rom 8:9). Let us then be careful to understand the importance of the Holy Spirit in our lives and in the church's life.

The Promise of the Holy Spirit

God promised to provide the Holy Spirit for every Christian. On the day of Pentecost, Peter told his audience, "The promise is for you, for your children, and for all who are far away, everyone whom the Lord our God calls to him" (Acts 2:39). That includes you and me.

John the Baptist said to the crowds on Jordan's shore that the coming Messiah "will baptize you with the Holy Spirit and fire" (Matt 3:11). Just before Jesus ascended to heaven, he said to his disciples, "See, I am sending upon you what my Father promised; so stay here in the city until you have been clothed with power from on high" (Luke 24:49). Jesus spent quite some time the night before his death explaining to the disciples the necessity of the Spirit's coming and what he would do for them.

Ten days after the ascension of Jesus Christ, the promised Holy Spirit came upon 120 disciples in the upper room, just as Jesus said he would. "All of them were filled with the Holy Spirit" (Acts 2:4). They came down from that place different from when they went up. Before, they were fearful, confused, and sorrowful. Now they possessed boldness, love, unity, and gladness of heart. Immediately, they were empowered to give an effective witness to Christ, and many thousands were converted.

Jesus had instructed them to tarry in Jerusalem until the power of the Holy Spirit came upon them. After that, the tarrying was to be over; they were to go out witnessing. It is inconceivable that a Christian would remain silent and idle once the Spirit of God comes upon him. Some people will not hold still long enough for the Holy Spirit to do anything with them. Others tarry too long and do not seem to get at the business of Christian witnessing. But the first disciples were obedient to the Lord, and they received the empowering he had promised.

In the upper room, the disciples were "all together" (Acts 2:1). Whatever adverse personal relationships may have existed as they trudged up the stairway to the room of waiting, those discordant notes were silenced as they subjected themselves to sincere prayer and honest confession. A sense of togetherness swept over the entire congregation. As they waited in eager anticipation, the room was filled with the sound of a mighty rushing wind; firelike tongues sat upon the heads of these people, and they spoke in other languages. The Holy Spirit had come! They were never the same again. He came like wind, blowing away the emotional excesses from their lives. He came like fire, burning out their moral impurities.

He came like a voice, giving the infant church a new language[1] and a new message.

When the Holy Spirit comes upon a Christian, that person will never be the same again. The Holy Spirit may not come in the same dramatic fashion as he did on the day of Pentecost, but the experience can be just as meaningful. The church was born in the upper room. The Holy Spirit has been continuously essential to its life and growth.

Throughout the book of Acts, we see plainly the importance of the Holy Spirit to the young Christian church. The Acts of the Apostles might well be called the "Acts of the Holy Spirit." Peter and John went down to Samaria after Philip had baptized many converts. "Then Peter and John laid their hands on them, and they received the Holy Spirit" (8:17). Cornelius, a just man of good report who feared God, also received the Holy Spirit (see Acts 10:21–35). Ananias found Saul after his conversion and said to him, "Brother Saul, the Lord Jesus, who appeared to you on your way here, has sent me so that you may regain your sight and be filled with the Holy Spirit" (9:17). And so it was. However, the Holy Spirit was not restricted to the apostolic days. Every Christian era needs him and is privileged to have him.

All great evangelists have been filled with and motivated by the Holy Spirit. At the funeral of D. L. Moody, C. I. Scofield said, "Moody was baptized with the Spirit and knew it. It was as definite an experience as was his conversion." Moody himself said, "The blessing came upon me suddenly like a flash of lightning. For months I had been hungering and thirsting for power in service. I had come to that point that I think I would have died if I had not got it. I remember I was walking the streets of New York. I had no more heart in the business I was about than if I had not belonged to

---

1. Editor's Note: The Holy Spirit supernaturally enabled the disciples to speak in the many languages of the Jews who gathered in Jerusalem for Pentecost. Occasionally, the Holy Spirit gives believers an ecstatic "prayer language." But the Holy Spirit does not confer this ecstatic language upon all believers, and those who receive such a gift are no more spiritually mature than other believers. (See 1 Corinthians 14.)

this world at all. Right there, on the street, the fire of God seemed to come upon me so wonderfully that I asked God to stay his hand. I was filled with a sense of God's goodness, and I felt as though I could take the whole world to my heart. This happened years after I was converted."

I can testify to this experience as well. I became a Christian at the age of eleven years. When I was turning sixteen, my mother passed away. Out of this experience, it seemed that God was calling me to a more positive witness and to a deeper committed life. At a public altar in a small frame church in western Kentucky, I knelt to surrender my life and talents—my all—to the Holy Spirit. Then and there the Holy Spirit came into and upon my life in such a way that I have never since been the same. Truly, I have experienced "righteousness and peace and joy in the Holy Spirit" (Rom 14:17).

Charles G. Finney once said, "He who neglects the command to be filled with the Spirit is as guilty of breaking the command of God as he who steals, or curses, or commits adultery. His guilt is as great as the authority of God is great, who commands us to be filled." Not only is guilt incurred, but also there is the great loss of the peace, poise, and power that rightfully belong to each Christian when one fails to be filled by the Holy Spirit.

The Need of the Holy Spirit

Why do so many people venture into the Christian religion and later withdraw or else enter into a stagnated experience? I believe such folks have gone the first mile but not the second mile. They have received Jesus Christ as their personal Savior but have not asked for and received the fullness of the Holy Spirit.

I can remember the days of the kerosene lamps. A lot of inconveniences were associated with them. We had to clean and fill the lamps, trim the wicks, and carry the lamps from room to room wherever they were needed. Then electricity came to our community. (We called it "the power" then.) The one-bulb, pull-chain fixtures suspended from the ceilings of our homes were a great advancement over the kerosene lamps. Now we push buttons or flip switches and bright lights come on. What a difference between the days of kerosene lamps and today!

This is somewhat like the difference between a Christian who lives without the Holy Spirit and a Christian who has the Spirit dwelling within. So many weak and spiritually defeated Christians are like soldiers fighting with spears and arrows when they have modern weapons at their disposal. They are like construction workers using wheelbarrows to build a highway or construct a dam when they could use massive earth-moving equipment. Many people live on the fringes of God's blessing and only enjoy fringe benefits. It need not be so. Failure in the Christian life is so often the result of failure to live immersed in the Holy Spirit and to walk in the Spirit.

E. Stanley Jones was a strong advocate of living in the Holy Spirit. To him, the Holy Spirit made the difference between living on the low levels and living on the high levels of Christian faith. He said, "I came to Christ bankrupt...By grace was I saved through faith.... I walked in the joy of that for months and then the clouds began to gather.... I wondered if this was the best that Christianity could do—to leave one in this divided condition? I found to my glad surprise the teaching concerning the Holy Spirit...I surrendered and accepted the gift by faith. He did cleanse as a refining fire...I was no longer at war with myself. Life was on a permanently higher level. It was no longer up and down. The soul had caught its stride. I went on my way singing a new song. That song has continued. It is fresher today than then." [2]

Receiving the Holy Spirit

The first requirement for receiving the Holy Spirit is to be a Christian. In the New Testament, we notice that the Holy Spirit was granted only to those who had already believed on Christ. Peter

---

2. Stanley Jones, "My Testimony," in Charles Ewing Brown, *The Meaning of Sanctification* (Anderson, IN: Gospel Trumpet Company, 1945), ii.

said to the crowd at Pentecost, "Repent, and be baptized every one of you in the name of Jesus Christ so that your sins may be forgiven; and you will receive the gift of the Holy Spirit" (Acts 2:38).

The second requirement is to ask for the Holy Spirit. "Whatever you ask for in prayer with faith, you will receive," said Jesus (Matt 21:22). This applies to praying for the Holy Spirit as well as to other requests. Our Lord said, "If you then, who are evil, know how to give good gifts to your children, how much more will the heavenly Father give the Holy Spirit to those who ask him!" (Luke 11:13). The 120 disciples were praying in the upper room when the Holy Spirit came to them. They were seeking the Holy Spirit.

Third, a believer must consecrate himself to obey the will of God and be used by the Holy Spirit. "I appeal to you therefore, brothers and sisters, by the mercies of God, to present your bodies as a living sacrifice, holy and acceptable to God, which is your spiritual worship" (Rom 12:1). A sinner who comes to Christ is generally not ready to consecrate himself to the service of God right away. This person first needs—and seeks—forgiveness for sins. Afterwards, a new believer naturally desires to surrender to God for Christian service. Only then is the believer is ready to ask for the Holy Spirit.

Somebody once asked George Müller, the heroic Christian, the secret of his faith. He replied, "There was a day when I died, utterly died: died to George Müller, his opinions, preferences, tastes, and will; died to the world, its approval, or censure; died to the approval or blame even of my brethren and friends, and since then I have studied only to show myself approved unto God!" He consecrated himself to God. He died to himself that the Holy Spirit might live and reign within him.

"Do you not know that you are God's temple and that God's Spirit dwells in you? If anyone destroys God's temple, God will destroy that person. For God's temple is holy, and you are that temple" (1 Cor 3:16–17). The Spirit of God will not inhabit an unclean and rebellious physical body. The body must be clean and consecrated. This means that self must be surrendered and placed at the disposal of the Holy Spirit.

Next comes the act of faith. After we have asked for the Holy Spirit and consecrated ourselves to God, we should accept the Holy Spirit by faith. God's promises are sure. There is no greater blessing that God desires to give his children than the Holy Spirit.

The Holy Spirit may come to us in various places. He came to the apostle Paul at a house in Damascus. He came to D. L. Moody on the streets of New York. Charles Finney was in his law office. F. B. Meyer was walking down a lane. The 120 disciples were in the upper room. Countless numbers have found the Holy Spirit at a public altar of prayer. This was true with me. "Search, and you will find" (Matt 7:7).

The way for a Christian to find and receive the fullness of the Holy Spirit is so simple. Here are the simple steps: (1) Recognize your need of the Spirit. (2) Be obedient to God and walk in all the light you have on Christian truth. (3) Yield yourself to the Holy Spirit and diligently seek him. Finally, (4) accept the Holy Spirit by faith. Then the Holy Spirit will come. And what a difference he will make!

What the Holy Spirit Does for Us

We may use several words or phrases to describe the initial experience of salvation, including *justification, conversion, forgiveness, being saved*, the *new birth, believing in Christ,* and *accepting Jesus as our personal Savior.*

Likewise, Christians use several terms to describe the subsequent experience the Holy Spirit, such as the *baptism of the Holy Spirit, receiving the Holy Spirit, being filled with the Holy Spirit, entire sanctification,* and *Christian perfection.* Each phrase partially describes what happens when the Holy Spirit comes. Together they present a beautiful image of what takes place when the Holy Spirit establishes his throne in the heart of a believer.

However, it is not the term but the experience that counts. This experience results in purity, peace, and power in Christian living. The work of sanctification in the heart of the Christian by the Holy Spirit is very important to a believer's stability and spiritual success. Jesus asked the Father for the sanctification of his followers (John 17:17). Peter said that even though the 120 disciples were already converted, on the day of Pentecost God gave them the Holy Spirit, "cleansing their hearts by faith" (Acts 15:9). In this way, said Paul, even Gentiles could be "sanctified by the Holy Spirit" (Rom 15:16).

We can consecrate ourselves to God, but we cannot sanctify ourselves. We do the consecrating, but the Holy Spirit does the sanctifying. On Mount Carmel, Elijah consecrated the sacrificial offering, but God consumed the offering with fire (1 Kings 18:36–39). So is it when we consecrate our lives to God.

The Holy Spirit sanctifies the nature of the believer. Wherever he abides, he cleanses all that is around him. Sanctification does not destroy the human nature of the Christian; but it purges, untwists, and redirects the impure and warped aspects of our nature so that God can use us. When the Holy Spirit sanctifies, a life of holiness will naturally follow. Holiness has been alternately described as "wholeness." Indeed, the person who has been sanctified by the Holy Spirit is complete in Christ. Sins are forgiven; the life is fully dedicated to God; the perverted nature is cleansed; the Holy Spirit dwells within to do his holy work.

A child is as much a human being as is an adult, but he needs physical growth and mental development to become mature. So a person who is "saved and sanctified" is perfect in Christ, but she will naturally grow in the grace and knowledge of our Lord Jesus Christ. Sanctification is an immediate and definite experience; yet the Holy Spirit continues his cleansing and refining work throughout the believer's lifetime.

The abiding Spirit helps us to do what pleases God. Paul writes, "Those who are in the flesh cannot please God. But you are not in the flesh; you are in the Spirit, since the Spirit of God dwells in you" (Rom 8:8–9). Surely, if our lives are directed by God's Holy Spirit, they will be pleasing and acceptable to God. The Holy Spirit working within us assures us of our salvation (v. 16). He teaches us the Word of God (John 14:26; 1 Cor 2:13). He produces Christian fruit within us (Gal 5:22–23).[3] He provides us with "righteousness and peace and joy" (Rom 14:17). The Christian simply cannot afford to be without the Holy Spirit.

The Holy Spirit grants us power for Christian service. Jesus promised his disciples, "You will receive power when the Holy Spirit has come upon you" (Acts 1:8). Power! Isn't this the heart cry of every real Christian? But notice that this power has a purpose, and that purpose is to witness for Christ and serve him.

The power of the Holy Spirit may be expressed in various ways, but we see it most clearly in a victorious Christian life. Of the 120 disciples who received the Holy Spirit on the day of Pentecost, we hear further of only a few of them. What happened to the rest? We may assume that most of them returned to their homes and everyday occupations to serve the Lord and witness for him in their own unique ways. So the power that a Christian seeks is not that of an explosion—a flash, a loud noise, and then silence. It energizes us for Christian duty. The secret and source of this power is the presence and operation of the Holy Spirit.

The Holy Spirit at Work in Us

In Galatians 5:22–23 we have a list of the Christian traits that the Holy Spirit will produce in us. They are called "the fruit of the Spirit." They are granted to the individual for personal enrichment, for attracting others to Christ, and for serving the Lord. Let us briefly consider each of these Spirit-given traits.

The Holy Spirit will produce the fruit of love in the genuine Christian. You cannot adequately love other people without the Holy Spirit within you; on the other hand, you cannot help but

---

3. See the Study Guide for biblical background on the gifts of the Holy Spirit.

show love to others if you possess the Holy Spirit. It is the nature of a mockingbird to sing, and it is the nature of genuine Christians to love, "because Christ's love controls us" (2 Cor 5:14 NLT).

The Holy Spirit also brings us a harvest of joy and peace. Through the Holy Spirit, we have rest, assurance, security, and serenity of the soul. Peace and joy may be ours under all circumstances when the Holy Spirit dwells within and works within.

Patience will appear when the Spirit abides in our hearts. The Lord is patient with us (2 Pet 3:9). If you have him, this quality should be evident in you.

Another quality of the fruit of the Spirit is kindness. Can you imagine a Christian being any less than kind? One never has to apologize for deeds and words of kindness. And there is no rebuttal against kindness.

Goodness, or generosity, comes with the Spirit. When given the opportunity, the Holy Spirit will produce goodness in our lives. "The good person brings good things out of a good treasure" (Matt 12:35). The world has a right to expect goodness of Christian people.

The Holy Spirit also produces faith within us. Some translators use the word *faithfulness*, but faith and faithfulness cannot be separated. You cannot have one without the other. It is inconceivable that a person who is filled with the Holy Spirit would be anything less than faithful. The Holy Spirit is concerned with the mission of the church, and this mission can be fulfilled only by faithful believers.

The Holy Spirit will produce gentleness. Peter writes of "the lasting beauty of a gentle and quiet spirit, which is very precious in God's sight" (1 Pet 3:4). Unless gentleness is evident in the life of a Christian, that person's influence will be greatly lessened.

At the last of the list of the fruit of the Spirit is self-control. A well-controlled, temperate life will make the Christian a more effective witness for the Lord.

As we review this list of spiritual traits, we realize that the Holy Spirit works in the believer to bring about Christlikeness. Surely, every Christian should want the fruit of the Spirit. This is God's will. When we receive the Spirit, yield to the Spirit, and obey the Spirit, the Spirit's fruit will grow.

Living and Walking in the Spirit

"If we live by the Spirit, let us also be guided by the Spirit" (Gal 5:25). "Live by the Spirit, I say, and do not gratify the desires of the flesh" (v. 16). When the Holy Spirit takes control of our lives, we notice some immediate results. Yet he does much more after we receive him. A couple is married in an instant of time, but the marriage is a continuing relationship throughout the years. When a believer receives the Spirit, that person is sanctified, filled by the Spirit, and empowered by the Spirit. But for what?

The Holy Spirit is for usage, not storage. Jesus told his disciples that they would be his witnesses when the Holy Spirit came upon them (Acts 1:8). He told his disciples on the night of the Last Supper that when "the Spirit of truth comes, he will guide you into all the truth" (John 16:13). There is great joy in receiving the Holy Spirit and a continuing joy in walking in the Spirit.

We could say that the Holy Spirit is a spiritual antiseptic against sin. A physician's instruments are often sterilized and kept in a particular solution. By dwelling "in the Spirit," we have the assurance of victory over evil.

The Holy Spirit performs his work through the life of a Christian. Electricity can do wonders, but it must flow through wires or conductors. You and I are conductors of the Holy Spirit.

The Christian is the dwelling place of the Holy Spirit. "Do you not know that your body is a temple of the Holy Spirit within you, which you have from God, and that you are not your own?" (1 Cor 6:19). With the Holy Spirit, you have harmony; without him, you have havoc. With him, you have power; without him, you have weakness. With him, you have assurance; without him you have doubt.

Every Christian needs to be controlled by the Holy Spirit. Our Christian experience can be preserved only if the Holy Spirit rules our lives. Our service to the church and our witness for Christ will be ineffective unless it is motivated by the Holy Spirit. Jesus sent the Holy Spirit to his followers because he knew the Spirit would be essential to our victory and vitality.

Once a group of ministers were discussing whether they should invite D. L. Moody to hold a series of evangelistic services in their city. One commented sarcastically, "Does Mr. Moody have a monopoly on the Holy Ghost?"

"No," another minister replied, "but the Holy Ghost seems to have a monopoly on Mr. Moody!" Every one of us should pray that the Holy Spirit would have a monopoly on our lives as well.

Have you received the fullness of the Holy Spirit since you believed? If not, you should. He can turn your weakness into witness, your vacillating into victory, your doubt into assurance, your frustration into composure. When you receive him, you will have the high privilege of living and walking in the Spirit of Christ.

PERSONAL HOLINESS
By Gene W. Newberry

T he well-known British Methodist author W. E. Sangster wrote, "The purpose of God for man is to make him holy."[1] We affirm Sangster's position as a biblical and experiential truth and goal.

Hebrews 12:14 urges us to "pursue...holiness." The verb *pursue* has real force. Scripture challenges us to cultivate, to pursue, and to strive for holiness. Yet holiness is the gift of Christ, through his perfect sacrifice (Heb 9:13–14). This is not a contradiction, really. Christ has accomplished our redemption, but he does not impose it against our wills. We strive, yet we receive. We pursue, yet all is of grace. The point, however, is that we must not be indifferent to holiness. If we want an empowering faith, we must seek it and take steps toward it.

The Trinity

The doctrine of the Trinity is crucial for understanding the Holy Spirit's work, because it lays the broadest base for the divine activity. God is still creating and working. He is purposeful and powerful. Why do we need the Trinitarian formula to convey this, and how can we illustrate it? Where do the Holy Spirit and holiness come in?

The Trinity says that God is discovered in three manifestations and roles. He is, at the same time, Creator, Redeemer, and Comforter. Think of any man. He may be, at one and the same time, a son, a husband, and a father. Here we have a simple illustration of the potential range of personhood and the self. Likewise, God's

---

1. W. E. Sangster, *Pure in Heart: A Study in Christian Sanctity* (Nashville, TN: Abingdon Press, 1954), xi.

possibilities are infinitely multiplied through the Trinity. Holiness is conveyed through God, the Holy Spirit. The Holy Spirit is "God in action."

The main point to remember concerning the Trinity is that we are not talking about a speculative doctrine but rather an experiential one. The doctrine of the Trinity is literally forced upon us because it is the only way to explain everything that has been disclosed to us about activity of God. So there are three points of view from which one may think of God.

Note first that God's creatures look upon him as Creator and Sustainer. Note second that all who have been touched by his forgiveness and grace look upon him as Savior and Lord. Note third that those who have entered into the fellowship of his church lean upon him as the presence who calls, comforts, and sanctifies. Yes, we have three "points of view"—even three distinct operations—of God, but they are functional explanations and nothing more. God is finally only one, after all. We dare not suppose that he has parceled himself out among his various modes of being. The activities in the Godhead are not competitive ones, and the Godhead is not a committee. A proper Trinitarianism requires us to acknowledge that God works simultaneously and indissolubly as Father, Son, and Spirit.

The Creature and the Creator

When someone uses the word *holiness*, we should ask if the noun is meant to describe the holiness of human beings or the holiness of God. Both, of course, are appropriate. However, priority and ultimate truth are given to the fact of divine holiness. God alone has absolute uprightness, love, and power. All human experiences are derived and relative with respect to God. All that we have is a bestowal from God. The injunction in Leviticus and First Peter is that we should be holy because God is holy (Lev 11:44–45; 19:2; 20:7, 26; 1 Pet 1:16).

We often overlook one aspect of this truth: we are creatures and not the Creator. This means we are dependent upon God. Only God is capable of supernatural acts, while we are capable of natural acts. Take, for example, our prayer life. Prayer is a natural human expression of dependence and, in a sense, is not unlike our other natural activities such as working and eating. With respect to his nature as the eternal Father, God does not need to pray because he is totally self-sustaining and self-sufficient. Yet Jesus needed to pray because he was the God-man, and in his humanity he felt the need of the Father's guidance and support.

The doctrine of the Trinity also reveals the true nature of our faith. We sometimes assume that faith is sheer force, in which we clench our fists and grit our teeth and storm God's throne, beating on the door of heaven until our knuckles are bloody. But the divine Son's relationship with the Father reveals that faith is nothing like that. Faith actually is a relationship of trust that we sustain with God. It is our response to having been received by him. Faith is our acceptance of God's faithfulness. As Paul puts it in 1 Thessalonians 5:24: "The one who calls you is faithful, and he will do this."

Thus, everything we have and do and are, is derived and creaturely. So it is with our holiness. But we are capable of a supreme God consciousness, as Jesus was.

Divine Holiness

Let us affirm first of all that God is holy. This signifies his separation from, and transcendence over, all his creation. God's holiness is his supremacy, majesty, and awesome glory. It is the ethical spotlessness of his character. As P. T. Forsyth has said, "Everything begins and ends in our Christian theology with the holiness of God."[2]

How is the doctrine of holiness developed in Scripture? The primary emphasis in the Old Testament is that objects and places may be declared holy. They are not holy in themselves, but by virtue of their intended use and purpose, they are withdrawn from normal

---

2. P. T. Forsyth, *The Work of Christ* (London: Independent Press Ltd., 1934).

use and dedicated to God's service. Something of awesome mystery may surround such things that are "set apart." For example, sanctity enveloped the bush that burned before Moses' eyes, the ground became holy, and he removed his shoes (Ex 3:1–5). Uzzah was struck dead as he steadied the ark, symbolic of divine presence (2 Sam 6:1–7). The ark seemed to be loaded with "holy electricity." Such examples are impressive and constitute the first lesson in our appraisal of holiness.

Human beings were sometimes considered holy in this sense of being "set apart" for a special purpose. It was most frequently a ceremonial sanctity issuing from their devoted acts of consecration (Ex 29:29–33). It could, of course, have a deeper level of significance embodying ethical righteousness, shown most particularly in the experience of the prophets (Isa 6:5–7). But in the Old Testament, the term *holy* was applied primarily to things and places.

The development of this doctrine in church history has been both confounding and inspiring. The general developments and divisions are mainly four:

First is mystical and ascetic holiness. This was evident mainly in early monasticism, which held that a life of withdrawal from the world was holier than one of common labor or vocation.

Second is sacramental holiness, shown in its most pronounced form in Roman Catholicism's teaching that grace is objectively conveyed in the sacraments and meritoriously achieved in good works. As a result, Catholicism has a more formal doctrine of sainthood than any other religious group.

Third is positional and confessional holiness, wherein a Christian is considered holy by virtue of being raised to new life in Christ by the rite of baptism. This view still regards the believer to be inescapably sinful. However, a Christian is urged to strive for fuller sanctification through the various means of grace and obedience to the commandments of Scripture.

The fourth position on holiness—the one that has challenged the Church of God movement—might be called experiential holiness or Christian perfection. We teach a doctrine of purity of heart, realizable now through the power of the Holy Spirit and in communion with a God of love.

Divine Spirit, Son, and Father

Too many Christians think of the Holy Spirit in impersonal or subpersonal terms. Some writers will use the word *it* in reference to the Holy Spirit. However, the Spirit is not a thing but a person in the Godhead, like the Father and the Son. Personal pronouns are repeatedly applied to him (see John 14:16–17). Personal qualities are assigned to him (see 1 Cor 12:11). Personal acts are ascribed to him (see John 16:13).

Isn't it possible that an experience of the Spirit could be more real to us than an experience of either God the Father or Christ the Son? The abiding aspect of a human being is the spirit; this is a person's internal, indestructible self, made in the image of God. My spiritual self has attributes of personality (thinking, feeling, and willing), just as God has. In fact, this is the way God gets at me. He has made possible a relationship, a communion of spirit, between himself and me at this level, the deepest and most real of all. Any sensitive Christian can reflect upon this experience of God's Spirit dwelling within. In this vein, one writer has paraphrased Galatians 2:20 to read: "It is no longer I who live; the Spirit of Christ which is the Spirit of God which is the Holy Spirit lives in me." Yes, the Spirit can lead us back, and up, to Christ and God.

When all is said and done, however, the Holy Spirit is none other than the Spirit of Christ. The Holy Spirit came upon Mary, his mother (see Luke 1:35). He was visibly evident at Christ's baptism (see Mark 1:10). Best of all, the Spirit continues the work of Christ. If Christ is the content of the new life, the Spirit might be called the agent of the new life. Our Lord promised that "when the Advocate comes...he will testify on my behalf" (John 15:26). And "when the Spirit of truth comes...he will glorify me, because he will take what is mine and declare it to you" (John 16:13–14).

Thus, we are justified, sanctified, and sealed in both Christ and the Spirit. We have joy, faith, love, and communion in both Christ and the Spirit. This is why at times in Paul's writings it is hard to distinguish between Christ, the Spirit of Christ, and the Spirit. He says that to live "according to the Spirit" is the same as to live "in Christ" (Rom 8:1–9), and it is from Christ that we are to discern the true pattern of life in the Spirit.

What Happened at Pentecost?

Seven weeks after Easter, the church celebrates Pentecost. This is the festival of the Holy Spirit. It is clear from Acts 2 that Pentecost was a collective spiritual experience. It was for a group of believers, the "church to be." The Spirit came upon a united, worshiping, and expectant community of Christians. Notice how exactly their experience fulfilled the challenge laid down by Jesus in Luke 24:49: "And see, I am sending upon you what my Father promised; so stay here in the city until you have been clothed with power from on high." We are here confronted with the most tremendous commencement exercises in the Word of God. Pentecost is inauguration day for the church.

The church came into being on the day of Pentecost with a plentitude of power; this was the kind of inaugural the Spirit would give. It was the kind of beginning that the church needed. It was as though a dry riverbed suddenly filled to overflowing; later the water would come more modestly in the usual channels. Once would be enough for the two accompanying physical phenomena, the "tongues, as of fire" and "a sound like the rush of a violent wind" (Acts 2:2–3).

The closing verses of Acts 2 show the results of such an auspicious start for the church. Three thousand converts were baptized. They had all things in common. "Day by day, as they spent much time together in the temple, they broke bread at home and ate their food with glad and generous hearts, praising God and having the goodwill of all the people. And day by day the Lord added to their number those who were being saved" (vv. 46–47). These are exciting words even when we read them in the twenty-first century.

There have been two main opposing interpretations of what happened at Pentecost. The greater number of scholars has said that the gift at Pentecost was not that of historic language, but rather that of ecstatic, heavenly language. It was an incoherent babbling, or perhaps rapturous "hallelujahs," they say. This interpretation surely does not do justice to the meaning of the writer of Acts, Luke, in verses 8 and 11: "And how is it that we hear, each of us, in our own native language? ...in our own languages we hear them speaking about God's deeds of power."

Over against the "babble of voices" approach to interpreting the significance of Pentecost is the "linguistic and missionary" approach. Its main points can be stated briefly:

First, at Pentecost we have a temporary language endowment for evangelistic purposes. Over a dozen nations are listed in Acts 2 as being present at Pentecost. Even if most of these foreigners understood the two most common languages (Greek and Aramaic), the situation required a miracle of communication. It would appear that the gift of language was necessary if the assembled multitude were to hear the good news of God. The confusion of tongues was for the moment overcome and, in principle, abolished altogether. In simple truth, at Pentecost, the Holy Spirit accomplished a breakthrough of the language barrier.

Second, Pentecost brought spiritual empowerment for witness and outreach. "You shall receive power" was the promise. The New Testament Greek word for power is *dunamis*; it is a cousin of our English word *dynamite*. Young Christians needed power for devotion and love to Christ, but also power for service. When the Holy Spirit came, they worked as if they were supernaturally possessed. The Spirit is the continuing dynamic in the life of the witnessing church and of its witnessing servants.

Third, Pentecost revealed the missionary character and universal outreach of the gospel. The Pentecost experience comes at the beginning of a great missionary book, the Acts of the Apostles. It describes how God's ultimate intention with respect to the world began to go into effect. Note the official missionary commissioning in Acts 13:2: "While they were worshiping the Lord and fasting, the Holy Spirit said, 'Set apart for me Barnabas and Saul for the work to which I have called them.'" The Spirit alone can prepare the world for Christ's mission. He alone is the great convincer. Since Pentecost, the church has the mandate to draw the entire world within the circle of light that is Christ's.

The Holy Spirit and Sanctification

In the Old Testament, it was mainly places and objects that were made holy; but in the New Testament, it is people who are known for their holiness. Jesus said that the pure in heart would see God (Matt 5:8). Paul held that it is the goal for Christians to be holy in life and character. God calls us to "sanctification" as he gives us his Holy Spirit (see 1 Thess 4:7–8).

When we talk about personal sanctification, we are describing a converted person who, through repentance and faith, has made a start in the Christian life. This Christian is at the beginning of a spiritual journey and wants to go further. This disciple needs to move past forgiveness to fulfillment—from being changed to being controlled. He needs something of continuing meaning. It makes good sense to the believer that there are now additional steps to be taken toward a higher life in the Spirit.

Dr. John Knox explains helpfully the extent of the sin problem when he writes, "This new life made itself known to him [Paul] as forgiveness and emancipation, as pardon from the guilt of sin and release from its power."[3] The new Christian needs an adequacy, an enabling, to become a victorious Christian and follow what Sangster calls "the path to the peak." Jesus promised the disciples that

---

3. John Knox, *Chapters in the Life of Paul* (New York: Abingdon-Cokesbury Press, 1950), 141.

they would receive such power when the Holy Spirit came upon them (see Acts 1:8).

Two extremes of doctrine concerning sanctification can be troublesome. One is that we so overstate the initial experience that it becomes a glorified "spot" that the Christian never moves beyond; the sanctified believer does not realize any need to grow in sanctification. This pilgrim has had the "second blessing" and that is the conclusion of the matter. The second extreme is to teach that there is no "spot" at all; the young Christian is left to expect no transforming encounter with the Holy Spirit. Obviously, this is much too casual an approach, both in the light of scriptural promises and our experience of the need for greater depth and quality in the Christian life.

Many feel that the best title to give this depth experience in the new Christian is the "infilling of the Holy Spirit." Other terms are also biblically sound. The crucial point is that sanctification is better explained by what is put into the personality than by what is taken out. Our passions and instincts are divine endowments. They have great potential for good or ill. We cannot eliminate them, but we can cleanse, harness, and govern them by the enabling of the Holy Spirit.

What about carnality, our natural bent to sin and sensuality? Does sanctification remove our carnal nature, or cleanse it, or change it in some other way? Here again we need to be sure of our definitions. Sin is not a thing that can be quantified; rather it is a relationship, a rebellion against God, a refusal of his love. Human carnality is overcome most effectively by crowding it out through love. Here again is the helpful concept of the Spirit's infilling. Paul says that "God's love has been poured into our hearts through the Holy Spirit that has been given to us" (Rom 5:5). Acts 2:4 explicitly states that at Pentecost the disciples "were filled with the Holy Spirit." Paul charges the Ephesians to "be filled with the Holy Spirit" (5:18).

It may surprise some that holiness turns more on the presence of love than it does on the absence of sin. This is the truth that John Wesley saw. The Holy Spirit inhibits sinful tendencies by the rule of love in the heart. It is the picture of love conquering sin, love filling the heart, love taking up the whole capacity of the soul. Personality has sturdy roots. If our human traits could be dug out, we would no longer be human. Instead our personalities receive the engrafting of love so that we can produce a fairer, finer fruit—namely, the fruit of the Spirit (see Gal 5:22–25).

Let's be aware of another danger: While sanctification may not be seriously questioned in a local church, it may no be seriously preached and practiced either. The test of it comes with the pastor, the teacher, the parent, the counselor. Will they present the doctrine earnestly, and will they provide opportunities and encouragement for it to be experienced?

Holiness teaching must deal at scholarly depth with a couple of key words. The Greek word for *holy* in the New Testament is *hagios*. (The verb is *hagiadzo*, meaning "to sanctify.") In its technical and ceremonial meaning, the word signifies something that is separated for a purpose—that which is claimed, set apart, and possessed by God. Clearly, God intends that these ceremonial meanings be translated and elevated into experiential meanings. The second key word is *teleios*, which is translated in many English versions as *perfect* and *perfection*. It means "to complete, to mature, to make whole." This word refers to the perfection of a person's intention and desire. We are not faultless before God, but our intentions may be blameless. Here again we may receive a fine insight into human possibilities and God's promise for our spiritual health and wholeness. These biblical meanings need to be translated into current, relevant, practical applications.

Based on Relational Theology

Perhaps we can best apply the doctrine of sanctification in our local congregations if we realize that holiness theology is basically relational theology. What do we mean by this? It can be stated briefly: When God created human beings, he made a relationship with them. Sin fractured this relationship. The atoning death of Christ restored the relationship. The church nourishes it, and the Kingdom implements it. The resurrection of our bodies will guarantee the continuation of God's relationship with us.

So we are called to a new height of moral relationship with a holy God. Our sin and rebellion have been an affront to God's holiness. The young Christian is called to God and becomes a child of God, a relationship that requires moral obedience to God. This is made possible through our Lord's sacrifice of himself on the cross, which accomplishes our forgiveness and renewal. We can never understand adequately the meaning of holiness until we reaffirm the meaning of conversion. Here we meet Christ with repentance and faith to receive his forgiveness and become new spiritual creatures.

Beyond conversion there is a distinct and separate experience of divine infilling, which imparts God's own moral likeness and strength. Sanctification does not cancel out our humanity; rather, it supercharges our moral capability by imparting a plentitude of love and power. We are called to the righteousness of God, which depends on faith in him (see Phil 3:9). In sum, God calls us to sanctification. It is a "plus" experience. It is for the Christian. It has a definite beginning and is capable of infinite increase.

Clinical Meanings

We have in holiness theology both confessional and clinical meanings to understand and seek. Three more key words take us to the center of this truth. Paul indicates in Romans 5:5 that "the love of God" is poured into our hearts by the Holy Spirit. That is the first word, *love* (Greek, *agape*).

Luke says in Acts 1:8, "You will receive power when the Holy Spirit has come upon you; and you will be my witnesses." That is the second word, *power* (Greek, *dunamis*).

The third word is used by our Lord frequently in the fourth Gospel. Jesus said he would send the *paraclete*, the "Comforter," which is another term for the Holy Spirit. All too often we infer that the Comforter is someone on whose shoulder we cry in time of sorrow. This solace is indeed available to the Christian. However, the word *paraclete* is much stronger and has greater range. He is the one whose presence gives us adequacy for righteous living. The *paraclete* identifies with us and stands beside us. He is our advocate when we face any trial. He bears arms beside us when we are in battle. This great truth has been too long overlooked by holiness theologians.

The doubters of holiness keep asking, How can this high experience be possible for mere mortals? The answer is that the Holy Spirit—as love, as power, and as presence—can enable anyone to qualify for sainthood. This fills out what we are trying to say about the experiential meanings of this doctrine. Christian holiness is deeply personal and dynamic. It calls us to the pinnacle of religious truth and challenge.

Add to this the fact that we are not saints in isolation. As Paul indicates in 1 Corinthians 12:13, "In the one Spirit we were all baptized into one body…and we were all made to drink of one Spirit." God brings us into the community of faith, the *koinonia* of the Spirit. We are placed by conversion and the Spirit's infilling into the Christian community of sharing, participating, and serving. We find here the complete personal meanings of holiness and affirm the bedrock truth of our spiritual quest.

This makes the doctrine of holiness not only one of deep personal experience and witness but also one of corporate meaning and dedication. It moves quickly past the limitations of propositional and ceremonial holiness to that of experience and service. Far from being a doctrine of limitation and embarrassment, this doctrine reveals our very reason for being. It makes a major contribution to Christian life and thought, indeed to ecumenical thought. There is a wistful yearning across the Christian world for a new depth of spirituality and an empowering faith. However, this yearning cannot be fulfilled by a mere verbalizing of theological formulas. It requires authentic renewal and commitment to respond to the needs of the world.

The Complex Predicament

Holiness people must deal with several difficult problems. We have had extremists stating our case. We have tried the ethics of easy answers. We have attempted to overpower each other with strident theology and oratory. We have too often judged and scolded any who were not in total agreement with our definition of holiness orthodoxy. We have often been our own worst enemies.

Holiness people often underestimate the complexity of the human predicament. We do not face the problems in this present world in a tough-minded way. We are guilty of promoting cheap grace, failing to realize that it is impossible to define holiness in merely negative terms. We cannot define the holiness position by outlining how to avoid moral contamination. We live in the very real historical world. It is a world on fire, a world gone mad, a world falling apart.

Therefore, we must avoid asceticism, legalism, and social isolation as we state the holiness position. We are talking about a total commitment. We are talking about a quality of heart and life. We are talking about a penetration of love and power, just as the apostle Paul and John Wesley did. Wesley proposed it somewhat as follows: Holiness is not so much the absence of sin as presence of love. It is the total inhibiting of sinful tendencies by allowing divine love to rule in our hearts. It is love excluding sin, love filling the heart, love taking up the whole capacity of the soul.

In summary, holiness is our reception of God's righteousness. The way of holiness is from the Father, by the Son, through the Spirit, to the Christian. It is not achieved by ourselves, but bestowed by Christ. It is an ever-dynamic relationship with God in Christ through the Holy Spirit. We are called to sainthood, but this is not an artificial sainthood. As the apostle Paul describes it, saint-hood means that someone lives moment by moment in complete dependence on God and dedication to God. It means that our con-secration is consecutive and perpetual. It means that we present ourselves—our unique personalities—as living sacrifices, holy and acceptable to God. Such an understanding of holiness leads us to the definition Paul gave of the Kingdom. He said it is not eating and drinking but righteousness, joy, and peace in the Holy Spirit (see Rom 14:17).

We need a new focus for the Hebrew word *qadosh* and the Greek word *hagios*, both meaning "holy." Their biblical contexts make clear that they do not describe a forensic or theoretical change of spiritual status. They describe a high relationship with God. They speak of nearness to God, dependence upon God, ser-viceableness to God, employment by God, commitment to God, and full conformity to his will. Admittedly, this is difficult for many people to imagine; it is heroic Christianity. Yet it is the calling of every Christian.

The Wind of God

The New Testament word *pneuma* is translated "wind, breath, spirit." We are told that the Spirit of God brooded over the pri-meval chaos and brought order out of it (see Gen 1:2). Such has been preeminently the Spirit's work ever since Creation—bringing harmony and order out of chaos. Whether in a gentle breeze or a wind of cyclonic force, the Spirit of God is still moving over God's world and God's people. It lifts us and buoys us up. It surrounds us like the atmosphere. It fills and occupies our personalities.

In one of her books, Anne Morrow Lindbergh tells of a round-the-world flight with her famous aviator husband. On one lap of the trip, they were stalled for some days. There was a complete calm—no wind into which they could direct their heavily loaded plane for takeoff. They waited for the wind. Finally, one morn-ing she was awakened from sleep by a rattling of the windows and shutters. She shook her husband and exclaimed, "Listen! The wind!" They quickly were airborne and on their way to complete their journey.[4]

One wonders if those Christians at Pentecost might not have blurted out to one another, "Listen! The wind!" We know that the Spirit's coming gave the apostolic church its life on wings.

Acts 2:4 states that at Pentecost, the disciples "were all filled with the Holy Spirit." The Spirit of God continued to fill and empower Christ's disciples (see Rom 5:5; 1 Cor 3:16; Eph 5:18). True, the Spirit's work is modified by our capacity. It apparently can be tailored by God to every believer's need. Yet it seems to be capable of massive openness and enlargement.

The Spirit's work is a many-splendored thing. The Spirit calls and convinces us of sin. He claims us as the new creations of God. He charges and controls us as committed and obedient children of the Father. From that point, the joys and victories of the Spirit-filled life can be continuous and consecutive. This is the essence of Christian holiness.

---

4. Anne Morrow Lindbergh, *Listen! The Wind* (New York: Harcourt, Brace and Company, 1938).

DIVINE HEALING

Dewayne B. Bell

Steven was a crippled five-year-old boy suffering from a bone condition that had affected him since birth. His mother was with him as he made his way on crutches up the walk to a home where some of his church friends had gathered for a small-group meeting. The other children were fascinated by the heavy brace on his better leg and the little shoe built up with four inches of extra sole on his withered short leg.

His pastor's wife greeted him with an understanding smile and introduced him to the rest of the group. "You know, children, Jesus is able to heal all our diseases," she said. The children looked with wonder at Steven's crippled body. Could Jesus really heal a leg that was four inches too short and the bone condition that had caused it? But she asked them, "Would you like for us to pray that God will heal Steven?" They nodded their heads and joined hands around the room while the pastor's wife anointed Steven with olive oil and prayed that he would be made completely well. Then she said to Steven's mother, "Tomorrow morning at eleven o'clock, I want you to measure Steven's leg and let me know how much it has grown."

Here were all the elements for divine physical healing as the church has experienced it for more than nineteen hundred years: the need of a sick body, the trust of the needy person, believers agreeing in prayer, and a gracious God to whom healing is the "children's food" (Matt 15:26). In Moses' day, God said to his children, "I am the Lord who heals you" (Ex 15:26). In David's time, God revealed himself as one who "heals all your diseases" (Ps 103:3). And Isaiah tells us that "by his bruises we are healed" (53:5).

Our God is a healing God, and when he sent his Son into the world, he appeared as a healing Savior. It was only natural then that the church of the New Testament would have a broad and active ministry of healing. As the body of Christ in the world, it continued to cast out devils, heal the sick, and proclaim deliverance to captives, just as Jesus had done in his earthly ministry. The book of Acts refers more often to divine healing in the apostolic church than the book of Mark refers to divine healing in the ministry of Jesus. We dare not question the fact that physical healing formed an integral part of the ministry of Jesus and of the early church. And divine healing continues to be a basic part of the ministry of the Church of God in the world today.

Increased psychological knowledge and better understanding of psychosomatic illness have caused some people to assert that the healings of Jesus and the apostles were simply spiritual and psychological reorientations that relieved a sufferer's psychosomatic symptoms. It is true that the restoration of person's life to wholeness is a greater miracle than the restoration of a limb to strength and usefulness. But when we talk of divine physical healing here, we are not discussing the relief of psychosomatic symptoms.

Was Steven Healed?

So what about young Steven? If he was healed, something must have happened organically. Here is what actually happened after Steven was prayed for a few days before an Easter Sunday.

Nothing unusual seemed to happen at the time Steven was anointed and prayed for. He had a good night's sleep, and his mother awakened him the next morning. He did not want to put his brace on, and she kept reminding him. Then he suddenly stood up. She reached out to help him, for he should have fallen over. Instead he joyfully walked across the room with no sign of a limp. God had extended his leg a full four inches overnight. There has been no recurrence of the Perthes disease that had caused the damage.

I asked him, "Steven, did you believe God would heal your leg that night when you went to bed?" Without hesitation, he nodded his five-year-old head and said, "Uh-huh!"

Is Divine Healing Neglected by the Church?

When he heard that I had been assigned to write on this subject, a friend said, "Oh, I'm glad we're beginning to teach divine healing again." Many feel that the church has lost much of its concern for divine physical healing. Is this true? Has divine healing been neglected by the Church of God?

We once expected all Church of God people to trust God for their physical healing. The evangelists of the church and local pastors often were called to pray for the sick. Some of our congregations remember that a wonderful series of miraculous healings marked the start of what is now a healthy church. Healing services at our regional and national meetings were well attended. Healing services at the convention in Anderson, Indiana, were listed in the program. Hundreds of sick and infirm were anointed and prayed for in these meetings, and healings frequently took place on the convention grounds between services. The Church of God moved against the current in those days, for mainline churches generally taught that the day of healing miracles was past. Bible-believing Christians had to look outside their own communion to find someone who would pray the prayer of faith for them.

How different the picture is today! Charismatic and neo-Pentecostal evangelists who hold healing campaigns are well known. Mainline denominations now have healing services as part of their regular ministry. Eminent physicians have shown persistent interest in the subject of divine healing.

In our own movement, authenticated healings may number in the thousands every year. Of the many Church of God ministers and laypersons whom I have interviewed concerning healing, not one failed to share a gripping testimony of divine healing.

Some told me of a very strong emphasis on healing in their local churches.

True, our emphases have changed. In sermons on healing, we hear less stress on staying away from the doctor and more on staying close to God. Church of God people are less inclined to judge someone who does not receive healing at once. At the same time, we have a much greater awareness of the emotional and spiritual bases for much physical suffering.

There is, however, a real danger in our current tendency to accept aid and insight from medical and psychological experts. The danger is that we may come to seek assistance only from human sources rather than from God, who is the true source of all healing. Most ministers have offered a prayer of faith for one who was ill, only to have the sick person continue describing the prognostications of the doctors and the warnings of the surgeons. Such a person has no faith for divine healing. The patient's eyes are on the illness, not on the Healer. The sufferer's faith is in his doctors and their medicine, not in the Great Physician. A person like this needs loving guidance to see the need for true faith in God.

Let's face it: What some sick people really want is not healing but attention and sympathy. We should avoid a bedside manner that caters to such falsity. The person may truly need friendship and the attention of the church, but these things should be shared in healthy ways—by participating in the quest for healing rather than a quest for sympathy. Christian compassion will always be a part of ministry to the sick, and we must not become judgmental concerning those who are ill. But a faithful Christian who is ill will look to God and his loving power to heal. The greater a believer's awareness of God's love, the less that person will need solicitous sympathy.

No, healing is not on the wane in God's church. The church is actually experiencing a resurgence of emphasis on divine physical healing in our day. This is as it should be, for God is our Healer. He "heals the brokenhearted, and binds up their wounds" (Ps 147:3).

Is Healing for You?

What about divine healing in your life? Since God is the creator and sustainer of your body, he has the power to make and keep you healthy. God himself has placed within us a deep desire for physical strength and health. The Bible teaches us that the body is the temple of the Holy Spirit (1 Cor 6:19), so God desires to provide the strongest, healthiest temple possible for his Spirit.

The Son of God suffered greatly during his earthly ministry, but we can never think of him as sickly, diseased, or physically frail. God wants all of his children to be strong and well. If there are valid exceptions to this, they are just that: exceptions. The New Testament norm is physical health for the spiritually regenerated. Read the Gospels again, taking special note of the varied and frequent encounters of Jesus with physical debility. What did he do when he met the lame, the leper, the blind, or those who could not speak? In each instance, his response was essentially the same: he healed them. Not once did he send someone away hobbling, stumbling, or mumbling without the physical healing that had been requested.

Christ is a healing Savior. Is he your Savior? If your Christian experience does not include physical healing, can it be that you do not expect him to heal you?

Let me give you another example of healing faith. This one comes from South Africa, where a young Christian woman was to have her leg amputated. It was nothing but a cold, withered burden. But God came to her in a dream and promised her healing. She called a friend and they took a train to another town where a local pastor's wife anointed and prayed for her. Instantly, while they were praying, life and strength flowed into the woman's withered leg and she jumped up and began praising the Lord. Then she asked her friend for the new shoe and stocking she had brought along for just this moment. She put them on and insisted on walking the half mile back to the railway station.

But you say, "God has not spoken to me in a dream." He has done better than that! He has spoken to you in his Word. "Are any among you sick? They should call for the elders of the church and have them pray over them, anointing them with oil in the name of the Lord. The prayer of faith will save the sick, and the Lord will raise them up; and anyone who has committed sins will be forgiven. Therefore confess your sins to one another, and pray for one another, so that you may be healed. The prayer of the righteous is powerful and effective" (James 5:14–16). This is God's word for you. This is his command to you. This is your privilege. This is your promise.

The husband of a young Indianapolis woman came to us on the Anderson convention grounds to tell us that his wife was seriously ill in their trailer in the grove. He was on his way to call the doctor, but I took another minister and went immediately to where this child of God had called for the elders of the church. After we had prayed the prayer of faith, we left—and so did the suffering. The doctor never got there, and she attended the general service that evening. She did what God told her to do, we did what God told us to do, and God did what he promised to do.

God is a healing God, his Son is a healing Savior, and God's church is a healing church. Christian hospitals began in ancient Rome and still set the standard for all institutions of healing. Nursing began with Christian women at about the same time. But the church has never lost sight of the fact that, though its doctors can dress the wounds and its nurses can care for the sick, God heals, and he alone. Just as Jesus paused often to speak the healing word to one in need, so the body of Christ includes the work of healing in its ministry. It should never be necessary for members of God's church to go outside the fellowship of the church to find healing.

The Elders Are Church Leaders

Your pastor is an elder in the biblical sense, regardless of chronological age. Other earnest, faith-filled leaders in the local church are also considered elders because of their spiritual maturity and power. Some churches may appoint a board of elders; but even in congregations where this is not formally done, certain mature believers are recognized as elders. One of their chief privileges and responsibilities is prayer for the sick. Here is how one pastor of a thriving congregation describes the ministry of divine healing in that church:

> Divine healing is not a special emphasis in our congregation. Rather, it is the normal practice which our people have learned to experience anytime or anyplace. If we are having a work bee at the church and I ask a brother how he is, and he tells me of a pain or sickness in his body, I call one or two of our brethren, and we anoint and pray for him right there. On prayer meeting night, when the requests for prayer are given, we invite those who have needs in their own bodies to come to the altar of prayer, and we pray for them right then. While the leaders of the church are gathered around the altar, we remember the other requests for prayer.

Incidentally, this congregation often has to bring in extra chairs to accommodate the people who come to prayer meeting.

Another pastor showed me a special prayer room that is in use many hours of the week. People who have been healed are encouraged to spend time there praying for others who still seek complete healing. This church has published an attractive pamphlet telling of miraculous healings that have taken place in their church through prayer. Steven, whose story began this chapter, attends this church, and I have interviewed each of those whose testimonies appear in the congregation's pamphlet. They include a two-year-old girl, epileptic and mentally disabled. Extensive tests showed a brain tumor. She had been in a coma for three days when the pastor's wife, prayed for her. Before praying, she asked the girl's mother to prepare a bottle of milk. During their prayer, the little girl stirred and reached for the bottle eagerly. Not only did further X-rays show a scar where the tumor had been, but a changed brain-wave pattern indicated an above-normal mentality. In the past year, she has been one of the brightest children in the church's nursery school. Other authenticated cases of healing in this congregation include two cases of cancer and another case similar to Steven's in which a teen-ager's leg was lengthened and a diseased hip cured through prayer.

We believe the church is the body of Christ, and Christ is the Great Physician. So the church, the body of Christ, continues his healing ministry.

Why Does James Mention Sin?

We could say that your body is allergic to sin. Your best friend may be unaware of your sin or choose to ignore it, but your body will find you out! Hatred, selfishness, and jealousy may poison our bodies with their venom. This is why Jesus forgave the sin in the palsied man before he granted physical healing. Jesus assured his disciples that not all diseases are the result of sin, yet we do not usually expect to find health and wholeness of body where there is sickness of the soul. A wise spiritual counselor will treat in quiet confidence the sins that you confess and will help you to find full release from the guilt and power of them. Then God, who is "faithful and just to forgive our sins and cleanse us from all unrighteousness" (1 John 1:9 KJV), will just as faithfully give you the physical healing for which you ask in faith.

Some of our congregations have made effective use of prayer therapy groups. Here people with physical and emotional needs come together weekly to share their experiences and seek deeper insight into their needs. Psychological tests are available for those who want to understand areas of weakness in their spiritual and emotional lives. Christians find new health and power in such a fellowship of prayer and discovery. Such prayer groups are not a substitute for private prayer or for anointing and prayer in time of illness. But they can be an important part of the church's ongoing ministry of healing.

Christian psychologist William Parker talks about the four demons of fear, inferiority feelings, guilt, and hate, which must be cast out of our lives if we are to receive the healing we seek. In his book *Prayer Can Change Your Life*, he tells us that effectual prayer must include surrender and honesty, and we must be positive and receptive. [1] Dr. Parker is no theologian, but his thrilling stories of changed lives and healed bodies testify to the fact that James's injunction to confess our sins to one another is still being practiced as part of responsible Christian therapy.

Varieties of Healing Experiences

Experiences of divine healing are varied. No one can discern just how, when, or under what circumstances God is going to heal. But here are general observations concerning the ways in which prayer for healing are generally answered. These affirmations may strength your faith and encourage you to trust God for healing.

First, God is able to, and often does, heal instantly. A baby girl is desperately ill with pneumonia. A Christian elder kneels beside the little crib and, slipping one hand under the child's back while laying the other on the small congested chest, silently prays the prayer of faith. In moments, the waxy body of the child fills with visibly inrushing new life and she passes from coma into a natural sleep. Two hours later, as the doctor arrives to find the child sitting up in bed, bright-eyed and cheerful. God has instantly healed the baby in answer to the prayer of faith. [2] A very similar story of healing from pneumonia was shared by a Church of God pastor concerning his young son. In this case, the boy was conscious. As

---

1. William R. Parker and Elaine St. Johns, *Prayer Can Change Your Life* (New York: Simon & Schuster, 1991).

2. Editor's Note: The writer later explains that we normally need to prepare ourselves spiritually and take the initiative to appropriate God's promise of healing. However, God can heal a person who is unable to consciously participate in the process, as in the case of this baby.

the boy himself participated in the prayer of faith, the flush of new life infused his young body.

With few exceptions, healings reported by the Gospel writers were instantaneous. This may have been one reason why they were reported. Others who came in contact with Jesus or the apostles may have been healed at a later time, so no report was made of it. We do not know.

Second, healing may be manifested in a variety of ways. Some people report feeling intense heat, intense cold, or other sensations in their bodies that accompany the healing. Often a person who is being healed simply has a deep sense of God's presence and a comforting assurance that the work is done. Only the Lord knows why such variety.

Third, long-term chronic ailments are apt to take longer to heal than more critical, short-term afflictions. However, there are certainly exceptions to this pattern. Viola was a cancer patient who undergone surgery three times in two years. Her left kidney had been removed and a tube inserted in her right one. She became bedfast, with her stomach and back so swollen she could not wear her clothing. During this time of illness, she accepted Christ as her Savior. Her pastor's wife visited her, anointed and prayed for her, and by the time she left the pain and swelling had gone. Viola had an appointment with her doctor later that day, which she kept. She was thoroughly examined, and the doctor finally shook his head and wrote across the chart in large letters, "Cured." Instantly healed of a long-term, organic disease!

The pattern of healing is varied, but the reality of divine healing is assured.

What Must I Do to Be Healed?

It is appropriate to ask the question in this way, because the way we exercise faith for healing is strikingly similar to the way we exercise faith for salvation. As with salvation itself, divine healing calls for preparation, appropriation, and affirmation.

Preparation. The apostle Paul exhorted the Corinthian Christians as they went to the Lord's Supper, "Examine yourselves" (1 Cor 11:28). Likewise we should examine our spiritual health when we turn to the Lord for physical healing. Such self-examination is a normal part of our quest for divine healing.

Your preparation for healing should include reading the Scriptures in depth rather than breadth. Read the Gospel stories of God's self-revelation thoughtfully and imaginatively. As you read about Jesus' compassionate work, let your mind return with him to those scenes. Imagine you are looking into his eyes. See the expression on his face. Hear the crunch of the fine gravel as he walks toward you. Feel his touch upon your weakened body as you include yourself among the needy ones who came to him. Let every scene of the Bible become real to you. Let his pure eyes search the hidden corners of your heart for attitudes of peevishness, jealousy, and hostility. You cannot look unflinchingly into his eyes with lust, dishonesty, or hypocrisy marring your character. Ask Christ to forgive and purge it all away. He will! "O Lord, you will hear the desire of the meek; you will strengthen their heart, you will incline your ear" (Ps 10:17).

Appropriation. You need to take the initiative to claim God's promise of healing. Notice the specific things you need to do: "Call for the elders of the church and have them pray over [you], anointing [you] with oil in the name of the Lord" (James 5:14). Belief in divine healing is not enough. You must appropriate it for yourself. *Appropriate* means simply "to take as your own." God's plan for healing is just as real and complete as his plan for salvation. Like his plan for salvation, it must be appropriated before it will take effect in your life. Follow his plan for healing, and accept your healing in perfect confidence.

In this respect, faith is different from hope. All people hope to be healed in some way, but God's children have faith they will be healed. They believe God and appropriate his promise of healing, confident that his work is being accomplished in their bodies. Little

Steven believed God healed him when his faithful friends prayed for him. God allowed him to enjoy the natural anesthetic of sleep while he lengthened his withered leg four inches in one night. Hope is not enough. "Now faith is the assurance of things hoped for, the conviction of things not seen" (Heb 11:1).

Affirmation. Praising God was the natural reaction of those who were healed in New Testament times (e.g., Luke 13:13; 17:15). How good God is to all of us! So let us praise him. When the prayer of faith has been offered and we have done all that the Scripture instructs us to do to appropriate our healing, let us praise God!

"According to your faith let it be done to you" (Matt 9:29).

THE KINGDOM OF GOD
Kenneth E. Jones

When John the Baptist began preaching in the open country near the Jordan River, his message was, "Repent, for the kingdom of heaven has come near" (Matt 3:2). When Jesus came back from his forty days and nights of being tempted by Satan, his message was, "Repent, for the kingdom of heaven has come near" (Matt 4:17). Not long after this, when Jesus chose twelve disciples and sent them out to preach, he charged to preach the same message that the kingdom of God was at hand (Matt 10:7; Luke 9:2).

We are not much interested in kingdoms in most parts of the world today. And even if we were, why should we care about any kingdom that was being discussed two thousand years ago? What difference could that possibly make to us now?

If the kingdom of which Jesus and his disciples spoke was just one among the human governments of the world, then it makes no difference at all to us, unless we are interested in ancient history. But the kingdom of God, or the "kingdom of heaven" as it is sometimes called, is not just another human regime. Instead, it is an integral part of the amazing plan of God to save us from our sins.

What Is This "Kingdom"?

The kingdom of God is the moral and spiritual power of Christ in his work as Messiah and mediator between God and man. The rule of God is made manifest in this world through Jesus Christ's dominion over his follows. All those who submit to Christ's rule are the subjects of his kingdom. Christ sits on the throne of each heart that is committed to God's will and rule.

The fact that Jesus is king, in the strictest sense, of those who have consciously yielded themselves to his rule is only a part of the whole truth of the kingdom. Because Jesus Christ is the omnipotent God, he is King of all creation. "He is the visible expression of the invisible God, ruling head of all creation, because in him were created all things in heaven or on earth, visible and invisible, whether thrones or ruling powers, or rulers, or authorities; everything was created by him and for him" (Col 1:15–16, author's translation).

Everything was made by Christ and for his own purposes. He rules over all creation in his providential wisdom. He made the sun and the stars, set them in their appointed places, and established the orbits of all their satellites. He spoke the plants and animals into existence and ordered their interrelationships, at which scientists marvel. He made human beings and put us in the world for his own divine purposes. And he rules over all these things according to his own will.

Christ also rules over the kingdoms and governments of mankind. He is the Lord of history, as well as the Lord of creation. Upon his head are many crowns. He has demonstrated his power over the destinies of nations since the dawn of civilization, and will end all history with the final judgment of every person who has ever lived.

This general lordship of Christ is central to the biblical concept of the kingdom of God. However, in this chapter we will focus on the personal aspect of the reign of Christ. The New Testament emphasizes that Jesus the King rules in the hearts of all those who submit to the conditions for salvation and then submit wholeheartedly to his rule. What are the conditions and implications of our citizenship in this kingdom?

The Kingdom Foretold

The Old Testament points forward in many ways to the establishment of the kingdom of God. The phrase *kingdom of God* does not occur in the Old Testament anywhere; yet the idea expressed by the phrase is found there in many forms. This basic idea can be expressed by the related words *rule*, *power*, and *authority*. In one way, we can say that the Old Testament is the story of the way God endeavored to develop in the Israelites an understanding of his power and authority to rule over them.

This story began with the demonstration of God's power in Creation. It continued as God worked with individuals to help them follow him and do his will. It advanced rapidly with the call of Abram to leave Ur and become the father of a great nation. But this nation that followed the rule of God had its true origin as a nation when God used Moses to lead them forth from the land of Egypt "by a mighty hand" to Mount Sinai, where he gave them a law and a tabernacle, and from there into the promised land of Canaan. There they grew into a nation, chose a king, and took their place among the kingdoms of the world.

Yet Israel was a kingdom with a difference. God was the real ruler and had been all along, even before a human king was crowned. At least we can say that God ruled except when the wickedness of his subjects caused them to rebel against his dominion and do their own will. This is the real point of much of the history and prophecy of the Old Testament. God sent the Law through Moses to tell his people how they ought to live in obedience to his will. After the death of Moses and his successor, Joshua, God sent judges to remind them of God's will and draw the people back to obedience and righteousness.

When the kingdom of Israel was established, God expected the king to rule, not in his own right, but under the authority of God. The king was supposed to be the kind of man who would seek so earnestly to know God's will that God would be able to direct the people through him. Saul failed in this and became so willful that God was not able to continue using him. David was a different kind of man, so much so that God said he "followed me with all his heart" (1 Kings 14:8). In spite of his sins, which are honestly reported in the Bible, he was in intention the kind of king God desired. He sought to do the will of God at all times, and after he sinned, he humbly and tearfully repented. He sought to let God rule the people through him. This is why he is held up throughout the rest of the Bible as the ideal king. This is also why the Jews were promised a Messiah—an anointed king—who would sit on "the throne of David" (Is 9:7). As David had sought to let God rule through him, so the Messiah would establish the rule of God by his divine power and authority.

When David died, his son Solomon made an auspicious beginning as king, but then he drifted so far from the will of God that at his death the kingdom was divided permanently. The rule of God over his people was never again demonstrated so perfectly as it was in the time of David.

During the rest of the Old Testament period, God sent a succession of prophets to call the kings and the people back to full obedience to the will of God. God never ceased trying to establish his own divine rule, or theocracy, in Israel. Yet God did not force the people to obey him, since he always desires a willing obedience rather than a forced obedience.

The prophets more and more specifically pointed forward to a time when God would establish his kingdom. For example, Isaiah the prophet, writing more than seven hundred years before Christ, put it this way:

> For a child has been born for us, a son given to us; authority rests upon his shoulders; and he is named Wonderful Counselor, Mighty God, Everlasting Father, Prince of Peace. His authority shall grow continually, and there shall be endless peace for the throne of David and his kingdom. He will establish and uphold it with justice and with righteousness from this time onward and forevermore. The zeal of the Lord of hosts will do this. (Isa 9:6–7)

This is one of the greatest passages of the Old Testament and clearly expresses several vital characteristics of the Kingdom. The Kingdom is to be established by the power of God. The Son of God himself will be born into the lineage of King David and sit upon the throne of this kingdom (which, for this very reason, is called the "throne of David"). He will rule over a kingdom that has no end, neither in time nor in extent. For as Isaiah put it, "all the nations shall stream to it" (2:2b).

These Old Testament prophecies were all given long before the time of Christ. They were given by Jewish prophets to the Jewish people, who were the people through whom God had chosen to save the world. He had chosen the Jews partly because they were unusually responsive to his will and to his revelation. He helped them to drive the Canaanites out of their homeland because of their wickedness and gave it to the Jews (Deut 18:12). He then helped them to set up a plan whereby he himself could rule over them—whether through judges, kings, or prophets.

Yet God's ideal was never attained before Christ. The judges, priests, kings, and prophets all pointed forward to a future kingdom, to a time when God could truly reign in the hearts and lives of men and women. Even the reign of David, when he sat on a throne in Jerusalem, was not a perfect fulfillment of God's plan for ruling his people but only a fore gleam of the glorious kingdom that God foretold. The priests offering sacrifices in the temple foreshadowed the Great High Priest who would offer himself for the sin of the whole world. The prophets kept pointing to a future kingdom that would be far more wonderful than anything which had yet been imagined.

The Kingdom Established

As we have seen, Jesus came preaching that the kingdom of heaven "has come near." He had been born in fulfillment of the prophecy in Isaiah 9:6–7, to become the king of whom the prophet had spoken. Nathanael was not rebuked when he said to Jesus, "You are the Son of God! You are the King of Israel!" (John 1:49). In John 18:36–37, Jesus tacitly agreed that he was a king when Pilate asked him to identify himself. In 1 Timothy 6:15, Paul called Jesus "the King of kings and Lord of lords."

These passages are just a few samples of the way in which the New Testament declares that Jesus is the king of whom the Old Testament prophesied. But if Jesus is king, where is his throne? Where are his subjects? How can we get into this kingdom?

First of all, we need to understand that the kingdom of God is spiritual and not physical. In this respect, it differs radically from all the kingdoms of this world by not having a human king sitting on a great throne-seat. Instead, Jesus reigns in the life of each individual who lives for him. He does not rule over a particular nationality but over those who have been born again and are therefore "of the spirit" (John 3:6; Rom 8:4–6).

By saying that the kingdom of God is spiritual, we mean among other things that God, who is spirit (John 4:24), guides us and rules our lives by working in and with our spirits. A human king could try to control our physical bodies but could not control our minds and our spirits even if he tried. Yet that is exactly what Jesus does. Instead of being concerned primarily with our bodies, he controls our bodies through our minds and hearts. The spiritual power through which he does this is what makes us call his kingdom "spiritual."

It is also a spiritual kingdom because it is governed through the agency of the Holy Spirit—the Spirit of God. Jesus came preaching and healing in the power of the Spirit. He promised the church, through his disciples, that he would send the Holy Spirit into our hearts to serve as our personal comforter, companion, counselor, co-witness, convictor, and conductor (John 14:16, 26; 15:26; 16:7). The Holy Spirit is to be our helper in all the ways in which we need help. He sets the members in the kingdom in the way that pleases him (1 Cor 12:18) and fills them with love so that they will work with God and with one another. So the spiritual kingdom of God is the realm dominated by the Holy Spirit.

One of the hardest lessons for the Twelve and for the early church to learn was that God intended the gospel to be shared with the whole world and that the kingdom of God must therefore include people of all races and nationalities. The Jewish people had long thought of themselves as the only ones worthy of being called the people of God, so it was very hard for them to see anything else.

Yet Jesus died for the sin of the whole world (Rom 5:18). The death of Jesus purchased redemption for all people alike, whether Jew or Gentile, so that in God's sight our human ancestry makes no difference at all (Gal 3:26–29; Eph 2:11–19). All people, regardless of race or nationality, are given an equal opportunity to be a part of the kingdom of God.

This had been foretold by the prophets of the Old Testament. Isaiah had said that the Messiah would bring forth truth to the nations (42:1–4), that he was to be a light to the nations (42:6; 49:6), that he would sprinkle many nations (52:15), and he would bear the sins of many (53:12). Daniel said of the Son of Man, "all peoples, nations, and languages should serve him" (7:14).

Jesus himself promised the kingdom to all nations, including both Jews and Gentiles (Matt 25:31–34). This promise referred not only to the fact that all kinds of people could go to heaven but also to the fact that they could become citizens of his kingdom in this life. Jesus openly acclaimed the faith of a Gentile in his own lifetime (Matt 8:10). He asserted that in the judgment day some Gentiles would put the Jewish nation to shame (Matt 11:20–24; Luke 10:13–15). Jesus warned the Jewish nation that the kingdom of God would be taken from them and given to others (Matt 21:43), so many of them would not know the blessings of the kingdom (Matt 23:37–38).

The death of Jesus broke down the division between Jews and Gentiles (Eph 2:14) and left no difference between them, so far as the kingdom of God is concerned (Gal 3:28). This is why Jesus told his followers to go "into all the world" (Mark 16:15) and to "make disciples of all nations" (Matt 28:19–20). They were to be his witnesses in the entire world through the power of the Holy Spirit (Acts 1:8).

Thus, the kingdom of God includes all nationalities of people and not merely the Jews. It is a spiritual kingdom, rather than a physical, political, earthly kingdom like those established by human beings here on earth. Now we look at one further characteristic.

An Eternal Kingdom

Since God himself establishes the kingdom, it cannot be overthrown; it will be everlasting. The prophet Daniel had said, "In the days of those kings the God of heaven will set up a kingdom that shall never be destroyed, nor shall this kingdom be left to another people. It shall crush all these kingdoms and bring them to an end, and it shall stand forever" (Dan 2:44). In Isaiah 9:7, a passage previously cited, God promised to "establish and uphold it with justice and with righteousness *from this time onward and forevermore*" (emphasis added). Peter called it "the eternal kingdom of our Lord and Savior" (2 Pet 1:11).

When Jesus came announcing his kingdom, he performed miracles as signs that God was at work in the world. When John the Baptist sent some of his disciples to ask whether Jesus were really the One who had been promised by God, Jesus answered that he was fulfilling the prophecies of the Old Testament by the miracles he was performing. By God's supernatural power, he established an eternal kingdom in this world.

The kingdom of God continues to exist in this present world. Jesus, as eternal King, rules over all Christians (Matt 28:18; Eph 1:20–22; 1 Pet 3:22). One of the clearest statements by Jesus of this fact is Luke 16:16: "The law and the prophets were in effect until John came; since then the good news of the kingdom of God is proclaimed, and everyone tries to enter it by force." That is to say, the preaching of John the Baptist marked the transition from the prophecies of the Old Testament to the fulfillment of the New Testament. Jesus declared that the kingdom of God was then placed within the reach of all who were willing to press their way into it. The same idea is expressed into the parallel passage in Matthew 11:12–13. The kingdom of God exists here and now, because Jesus is reigning in the hearts of the redeemed. We need not look for any future fulfillment of the kingdom prophecies of the Old Testament.

A False Interpretation

Many false interpretations of the kingdom of God are popular in the Christian world today. For the sake of illustration, let us consider the teaching called dispensationalism. This extreme form of premillennialism is well-known.

Basically, dispensationalism is the teaching that God has divided human history into distinct periods called *dispensations*. In each dispensation, God deals with people in a different way. Each part of the Bible is applicable to a particular dispensation and to no other. The Scriptures' promises, warnings, and teachings do not have general application to all people at all times but only to those living in a particular dispensation. Without even trying to outline all the consequences of this basic assumption, let us consider how it distorts believers' understanding of the kingdom of God.

Dispensationalism teaches that the kingdom of God is not yet in existence. It states that Jesus came to set up his kingdom but failed to do so because the Jews refused to accept it. The establishment of the kingdom was then postponed to some still future time, and the church was set up as a temporary substitute. When Jesus comes again, according to this theory, he will not fail to set up the kingdom as he did the first time, but will impose it upon the world by force. This is the basic outline of the theory of dispensationalism. But it does not fit the clear teachings of the Bible, as we have seen.

Dispensationalism teaches that the kingdom has not been set up; but the Bible says the kingdom was established by Christ nearly two thousand years ago. Dispensationalism teaches that the kingdom of God is to be a physical kingdom, with Jesus sitting on a physical throne somewhere on earth; but Jesus flatly rejected such an idea and insisted that the kingdom of heaven is spiritual. Dispensationalism implies that Calvary marked a point of failure in God's plan; but Jesus said that it completed the plan of salvation for all sinners. This theory holds that the church was not part of the original plan of God but rather that it is only a temporary substitute for his kingdom. However, the Bible speaks of the kingdom and the church in practically synonymous language, and declares that the church is a part of God's eternal plan and purpose (Eph 3:10–11). Dispensationalism looks forward to the reward of wonderful material benefits in some future kingdom here on earth; but the New Testament points us to the reward of being in the very presence of God in heaven.

What Difference Does It Make?

Does our belief about the kingdom of God make any difference? Will it change our attitude in any practical way? Why should we be so concerned about different theories of the kingdom? It is true that some fine points of theology make no practical difference in the human life. Some aspects of kingdom theology might be considered more theoretical and academic than practical. Yet we need to be clear in our understanding of the kind of kingdom God promised and established.

It changes our attitude toward the Old Testament. Dispensationalism breaks up the Old Testament into parts and applies the message of each part to one period of history and to no other. This means that much of the Old Testament—particularly the prophecies— would have no application to our lives at all. This theory insists that most Old Testament prophecies are still unfulfilled and must wait for the second coming of our Lord. All of the prophecies of the kingdom of God are still unfulfilled according to this theory.

It changes our attitude toward the church. If the church is only a temporary expedient, a substitute for God's kingdom, then it is not the glorious provision of God's eternal plan that Paul called it in Ephesians 3:10. If the church is a substitute for the kingdom, then the glories of the kingdom foretold by the prophets were not completely fulfilled in the church Jesus built. If this is true, it casts a shadow over the spiritual blessings we enjoy in the church. The Church of God teaches that the peace, unity, and victory over sin and the devil which we enjoy as Christians in the church are perfect fulfillments of the Old Testament prophecies of such privileges— quoted in the New Testament and applied to the church established at the first coming of Christ. Yet our dispensationalist friends say we must wait until Jesus comes the second time to see these prophecies fulfilled.

It changes our attitude toward the death of Jesus. Dispensationalism looks upon Calvary as the failure of Jesus' attempt to set up his kingdom. It is said that Jesus offered the kingdom to the Jews, and when they rejected it by nailing him to the cross, he had no other alternative but to "stop the clock of prophecy" and go back to heaven to wait for another time to set up the kingdom.

Yet the New Testament clearly asserts that Calvary was not a postponement of God's plan, even temporarily, but an essential part of it. Jesus insisted that no one could take his life from him but that "I lay it down of my own accord...I have received this command from my Father" (John 10:18). The death of Jesus did not mark the postponement of anything! By his sacrificial death on Calvary, Jesus broke the power of sin and made it possible for us to be redeemed from the kingdom of darkness and taken into his own kingdom. "He has rescued us from the power of darkness and transferred us into the kingdom of his beloved Son, in whom we have redemption, the forgiveness of sins" (Col 1:13–14).

The Kingdom Is Now Set Up

It is important for this fact to be emphasized. In the Scripture passage just quoted, we see that Paul spoke of the kingdom of God not as something in the distant future but as now existing. He said that he and other believers had already been brought into the kingdom by the power of God in Christ Jesus. That was nearly two thousand years ago. So if the kingdom was already in existence in Paul's day, surely we cannot continue to call it "future," as the dispensational theory does.

Jesus also spoke of the kingdom of God as a present reality. Let us look closely at one of his statements:

> Once Jesus was asked by the Pharisees when the kingdom of God was coming, and he answered, "The kingdom of God is not coming with things that can be observed; nor will they say, 'Look, here it is!' or 'There it is!' For, in fact, the kingdom of God is among you." (Luke 17:20–21)

The Greek word translated "among" is sometimes translated "within." It is used only this one time in the New Testament and is therefore not fully understood. But it is clear that Jesus taught that the kingdom of God was already a present spiritual reality in the lives of his believers.

In John 18:36, Jesus confirmed this fact before Pilate by saying, "My kingdom is not from this world." Jesus was not in competition with Pilate or any of the other rulers of this world. Rather, Jesus rules over the hearts of people who believe in him. This is the sense in which he is king, and all Christians are his subjects.

Seek First the Kingdom

While Jesus walked this planet in his divine-human life, he looked for people who would believe in him and follow him. He called them to forsake the sin of the world and worldly treasures, to pursue the spiritual treasures of God. In the middle of his Sermon on the Mount, he spoke at length of the dangers and futility of worrying over the physical treasures of this temporal world. Then he said, "But strive first for the kingdom of God and his righteousness, and all these things will be given to you as well" (Matt 6:33). Morally speaking, the essence of the kingdom of God is righteousness. "For the kingdom of God is not food and drink but righteousness and peace and joy in the Holy Spirit" (Rom 14:17).

As Ralph Earle points out in his commentary on Matthew, we should first seek the kingdom and righteousness of God in our own lives and then seek to bring others into it. This means that we should spend our lifetime in the pursuit of the kingdom of God. As soon as we have found it for ourselves, we should begin helping others find it.

If you are not a Christian, you can become a part of this kingdom by being converted. Forsake your sins, ask God to forgive you, and believe that God in Christ Jesus does forgive you and make you his own. You can then enjoy the blessings of the kingdom of God, right where you are. And you can begin to help others find the same kingdom. Seek first the kingdom of God!

THE CHURCH OF GOD
W. Dale Oldham

W hy write more about the church when so much has already been written? Why write about the church when churches are found at most prominent intersections, both in city and countryside? Why write about the church when its history so intermingles weakness with strength and shame with glory? Why write about the church when the story contains much of failure as well as success?

I believe that I must write about the church because so many people do not understand its true nature, structure, and purpose. I write to awaken the church, arouse it to action, challenge it to discover and use its vast untapped potential. I write because Christ loved the church and freely gave himself for it. So the church must be of great eternal importance.

The people of God need to move forward together "like a mighty army" to contradict error, work for the redemption of mankind, and introduce to billions of people "the faith that was once for all entrusted to the saints" (Jude v. 3).

Not only does the world need to see the church "fair as the moon, bright as the sun, terrible as an army with banners" (Song 6:10), but the church needs to see itself—both as it is and as it can become. The church is the citadel of righteousness, the household of faith, and the missionary force that Christ expects to evangelize the whole world.

This Is the Church

First, then, let us identify the church in Scripture. At least seven times, the New Testament church is referred to as "the church of God." Note Acts 20:28, for example, where we read, "Keep watch over yourselves and over all the flock, of which the Holy Spirit has made you overseers, to shepherd the church of God that he obtained with the blood of his own Son." Notice that the Bible translators place no capital *C* in the word *church*. The New Testament refers not to "the Church of God" but to "the church of God." It is not the name of a particular movement or denomination but a common word meaning "family" or "assembly."

Note these passages also: "To the church of God that is in Corinth, to those who are sanctified in Christ Jesus, called to be saints" (1 Cor 1:2a); "Give no offense to Jews or to Greeks or to the church of God" (10:32); "What! Do you not have homes to eat and drink in? Or do you show contempt for the church of God and humiliate those who have nothing?" (11:22a); "For I am the least of the apostles, unfit to be called an apostle, because I persecuted the church of God" (15:9); "You have heard, no doubt, of my earlier life in Judaism. I was violently persecuting the church of God and was trying to destroy it" (Gal 1:13); "(For if a man know not how to rule his own house, how shall he take care of the church of God?)" (1 Tim 3:5 KJV).

Occasionally, the church is given other designations, such as we find in verse 2 of Philemon, where Paul refers to "the church in your house," and Hebrews 12:23, which speaks of "the assembly of the firstborn." In the closing lines of his Roman letter, Paul writes, "All the churches of Christ greet you" (16:16). Because the church is God's family, God's people, God's called-out ones, it bears his name.

But in these days of proliferating "churches" and denominations, sects and religious movements, it is hard to see clearly what the New Testament church was. There is such a difference between the ecclesiastical organizations that have been established in modern times and the true church itself. There were no denominations, no sectarian institutions, in the beginning. The division and rivalry came only as people lost the holy, loving Spirit of Christ from their hearts. Our present Protestant denominations have come into existence since the beginning of the sixteenth century. Many of them found rise through much-needed and worthy reform movements. Even though they separated good ideas from bad practices, they nevertheless did separate Christians (see p. 5).

At the Start

What was the origin of the New Testament church? We know that Jesus said, "I will build my church" (Matt 16:18). So he declared at the very start that it is his church, God's church, a church under the control of the Holy Spirit because it is of divine origin. In Revelation 21:2–3, we read,

> And I saw the holy city, the new Jerusalem, coming down out of heaven from God, prepared as a bride adorned for her husband. And I heard a loud voice from the throne saying, "See, the home of God is among mortals. He will dwell with them; they will be his peoples, and God himself will be with them."

The church was established by divine initiative according to divine plans. It was meant to be motivated by the Holy Spirit and to become a major factor in the lives of the redeemed children of God.

Don't confuse the New Testament church with a denominational assembly that meets down at the corner every Sunday morning, for the church is far more than that. The church is the entire "family of God." It is composed of all those—and only those—who have experienced the forgiveness of sin and received a new spiritual life through Christ. It is constituted by Christ and peopled by the "called-out" ones. It is the body of Christ, the bride of Christ, the household of faith, the fellowship of the saints. You can't "join" the church, but Christ can join you to it by his divine redemptive power. Church membership is not obtained through "joining," but through conversion, salvation, being "born again." No human authority can take you into or put you out of the New Testament church. Jesus said, "I am the gate" (John 10:9), so we enter the family of God only through him.

Acts 2:47 says of the early church that "day by day the Lord added to their number those who were being saved." Only the Lord can add to his divine body, the church, because only he knows our hearts.

Don't be deceived at this point: joining a denomination is not the same as becoming a member of the body of Christ. As was said, Christians are those who, through repentance for sin and faith in Jesus Christ, have "passed from death to life" by a spiritual work of regeneration wrought in their hearts by the power of God (John 5:24). You can't "join" a group such as this. No, you cannot "join" this church; you must be born into it by a spiritual rebirth. As Jesus said to Nicodemus, "You must be born from above" (John 3:7). Nearly a thousand years before Christ, the psalmist seemed to catch a glimpse of the spiritual nature of the church as he wrote, "And of Zion it shall be said, 'This one and that one were born in it'; for the Most High himself will establish it. The Lord records, as he registers the peoples, 'This one was born there'" (Ps 87:5–6). God alone keeps the membership book for his church.

It is sobering to think of the millions who presume to be members of God's church chiefly because they have joined a denominational organization, subscribed to a creed, passed catechetical examinations, repeated certain articles of faith, submitted to the ordinance of baptism, or signed a member information card. Remember, the Lord alone adds to his church, and he adds only those who have honestly repented, turned from their sins, and believed in Christ for salvation. No one else is in the church Christ built. I once met a young man who, in his anxiety to belong to the "right" church, had joined every denomination in his little town! Yet only as he gave his heart and life to Jesus Christ could he possibly become a member of the New Testament church.

When people organize a denomination, I suppose they have a perfect right to draw up a list of qualifications for membership in that denomination, but that is not the New Testament church. The only church described in Scripture is God's church, Christ's church, the church under the control of the Holy Spirit. Who then can presume to draw up another list of qualifications for membership in it or dare to offer an alternate way by which one can belong to the divine family of God? Members of God's church have been "saved," redeemed from iniquity, "bought with a price." They have passed out of death into life through the transforming power of God. Without such a spiritual experience, no one can belong to the New Testament church, regardless of one's denominational or ecclesiastical affiliations.

The Whole Family

The fellowship of the church is exclusive, but it is also broadly inclusive. Paul wrote, "For this reason I bow my knees before the Father, from whom every family in heaven and on earth takes its name" (Eph 3:14–15). So the church is a broad fellowship as well as a narrow fellowship, extending to heaven as well as earth. Wherever the redemptive, saving power of Christ has worked its transforming miracle, you will find the church. Wherever two or more of the saved gather together in the Master's name, you have the church. As Christians meet together in worship, praise, fellowship, and work, there is the church. They may meet in a chapel or in a private home, but they are the church—the fellowship of the saints.

You see, the church is not just a local association of idealistic people; it is the entire "fellowship of the saints." It is every community of the twice-born, every divine gathering of those "called out" (Greek, *ekklesia*). It is the universal and eternal family of the redeemed, whose names are written in heaven.

Nature of the Church

Let's think more carefully about the nature of the New Testament church. God's church is a holy church. That word, *holy*, frightens anyone who does not know its true meaning or has not experienced divine transformation in Christ. But what does the New Testament mean when it uses this word to describe the church?

Paul said that "Christ loved the church and gave himself up for her, in order to make her holy...so as to present the church to himself in splendor, without a spot or wrinkle or anything of the kind—yes, so that she may be holy and without blemish" (Eph 5:25–27). God's church is not holy of itself; it is holy through its relationship to him. *Holy* not only means "pure" but also "set apart," separated unto God.

John wrote to the early Christians, "Do not love the world or the things in the world. The love of the Father is not in those who love the world" (1 John 2:15). Since membership in Christ's church is predicated upon a love for the Lord so real that it has led to our total commitment to him, it is natural to expect Christians to live in full obedience to his holy will. As Jesus said to his disciples, "Those who love me will keep my word" (John 14:23). So to me it seems strange indeed to see professed followers of Jesus Christ living just as they did before they "joined the church." They are still greedy and selfish, still frequent places of poor repute, still tell off-color stories, still follow the lusts of the flesh. Jesus said, "You will know them by their fruits" (Matt 7:20). In this connection Paul wrote to the Roman church, "Do you not know that if you present yourselves to anyone as obedient slaves, you are slaves of the one whom you obey, either of sin, which leads to death, or of obedience, which leads to righteousness?" (6:16). Membership in the New Testament church begins with spiritual transformation and renewal in Christ. Old things have passed away and everything has become new. Your desires and affections, your ambitions and motivations have all undergone a divine change.

Christ had barely spoken to the little tax collector Zacchaeus before this tree climber blurted out, "Look, half of my possessions, Lord, I will give to the poor; and if I have defrauded anyone of anything, I will pay back four times as much" (Luke 19:8). Belonging to the "body of Christ" does this kind of thing to a man! Did such a transformation take place in you? Merely "joining a church" cannot produce such changes. It is wrought from within by the power of God. When a man is really "born of the Spirit," God causes him to desire fervently to straighten up his past life and get his accounts squared with his neighbors so they will also be squared with God. He finds himself apologizing to those he wronged, those against whom he spoke maliciously. Something in his heart urges him to return anything he stole and to do everything else within his power to firmly establish this wonderful new relationship with God and with people.

Paul thought of the church as the worshiping people of Jesus Christ, who met together in Jesus' name. You see, Paul saw the church as a channel, a kind of pipeline, through which God's redemptive purposes were being manifested to the world. Through the church, the world was shown "the wisdom of God in its rich variety" (Eph 3:10). Anyone should be able to see the glory of God reflected "in the church" (v. 21).

The Church Is God's

Paul did not see the church as a merely human agency or organization. He knew it is "the church of God." It is created to be like God, not only in name but also in spirit and purpose. Note that Paul does not speak of "the church of Corinth"; he always writes about "the church of God which is at Corinth." As previously noted, wherever the twice-born meet together in any nation or circumstance, on earth or in heaven, it is "the church of God." No wonder Paul was upset when some of the Corinthian Christians began to separate themselves into little clans, saying, "I am of Paul," or "I am of Apollos," or "I am of Cephas." He said, "Has Christ been divided?

Was Paul crucified for you? Or were you baptized in the name of Paul?" (1 Cor 1:13).

Neither are we baptized in the name of Paul or Peter. Nor in the name of Luther, Wesley, or John the Baptist. We are born into "the church of God," God's church, Christ's church, the holy fellowship of the born-again, the transformed of the Lord. True Christians will not separate themselves into cliques and clans, raising walls and barriers between themselves and their brethren. Rather, they will tear down the walls. They will do everything they can to bring God's sheep together that they may dwell in peace and unity in one fold, with one great Shepherd. True Christians hate division and work always for unity. True Christians will not boast, "I am of Luther," or "I am of Wesley," or "I am of John Knox." Such pride of heritage is divisive in its influence and effect. Let it be enough that we are of Christ, have been transformed by his miracle-working power and grace, and share in the blessed hope of seeing him someday to dwell with him forever. There is no place for sectarian divisions in the church of the New Testament. The true church possesses a unity of soul, mind, and spirit that transcends all barriers. The barriers must fall if we are to ever answer the prayer of Christ, "That they may all be one" (John 17:21). Division in the church is sin.

Those in the church are spiritual brothers and sisters. The church is a family, all of whom are children of God. God is our Father and Christ is our elder Brother. How sad when we see a church family whose members are in conflict and envious of each other, constantly in unholy, carnal competition with each other. Actually, an unforgiving Christian is not a Christian at all but a stranger to God's forgiveness. Jesus said, "If you do not forgive others, neither will your Father forgive your trespasses" (Matt 6:15).

When I was a youngster, we had a huge oak tree that gave welcome shade to our side yard in summer and from whose branches brown leaves drifted down when autumn's frosts had touched them. We used to rake the leaves into lines denoting the walls of a chapel. Then I, as the preacher, would hold forth before a "congregation" made up of children from the neighborhood. Here we played church for hours at a time. One wonders how many adults are still playing church! "I'm a Christian," they say, but sin still lingers and ungodly attitudes still persist in their lives. Paul said, "Anyone who does not have the Spirit of Christ does not belong to him" (Rom 8:9). The saints—the dedicated, purified, called-out people of God—manifest the spirit of Christ wherever you find them and under whatever circumstances. Nor does one member of the church ever say to another, "I have no need of you" (1 Cor 12:21).

The exclusive, competitive, sectarian clannishness manifested here and there by certain groups claiming to be the true church must be highly unpalatable to Almighty God. You will know the church of God because its people will manifest the Spirit of God. They will love with the love of God; they will forgive with the forgiveness of God. The forbearance of God will be seen in their lives, as will his patience. And no earmark more clearly identifies God's church than that of humility and meekness. Find God's true people and you will hear no bragging over size, affluence, buildings, budgets, or the presence in their midst of financially or politically affluent members. Instead, you will hear them give God all glory and praise for what he is accomplishing through them.

Will We Ever Get Back Together?

We believe that in these "last days," God is calling his people together. How can that happen? We know that the New Testament church is essentially one. That oneness begins to be seen in the manifestation of a divine spirit, which in turn results from of a life-changing experience in Christ. It grows out of a personal relationship between us and our Savior in which all sins are forgiven, life is turned around, and everything is made new. As people experience this transformation of their lives, God will bring them together.

I mentioned earlier that the primary New Testament Greek word for the church is *ekklesia*. Let us trace the meaning of that word for a moment. In the Septuagint (Greek) version of the Old Testament, this word was used to denote the assembled people of Israel, the congregation of Israel, or the assembled people of God. This is what it meant to the Jews. Everywhere *ekklesia* was used in the New Testament, therefore, the implication was that the church is the people of God. In the Old Testament, the *ekklesia* was a nation; but in the New Testament, the *ekklesia* is the family and fellowship of God's people. It is God's gathering of the born-again.

Secular Greeks of the first century called their ruling council the *ekklesia*. One commentator tells us that it was composed "of every citizen who had not lost his rights as a citizen." Well, today, the church—the holy *ekklesia* or family of God—is also composed of all those who have not forfeited their citizenship in the kingdom of God.

The Church Is the People

We do violence to the word *church* when we use it to refer to a building of brick, wood, or stone. We often say "church" when we mean "chapel" or "sanctuary," a place of meeting. Never once did Paul do this. He did not say "your house, the church," but rather, "the church in your house." The church is not the brick and mortar; it is the people who meet inside that structure of brick and mortar, it is the fellowship of the saints.

Christians were called "saints" in Paul's day because they were holy people—people who had set themselves apart for the service of God. They were different because they had been touched by God. In their hearts, the love of God was very real, very wonderful, and very effective. We have spoiled the word *saint* by connecting it with halos, hermits, and ascetics, or with absolute perfection in judgment as well as attitudes and actions. But in the New Testament sense, the word *saint* just means a person in Christ, a redeemed person, a Christian personality, one who walks daily with the Lord and obeys his will, one who lives according to God's divine purposes for his life. A Christian saint lives in the world but is not worldly.

What do the "saints" do? Paul said that the church is the body of Christ and that Christ is the head of that body. Certainly, the body of Christ should be expected to do the work of Christ. So the church is an evangelizing force operating through the Holy Spirit to win the world to Christ. The church is the visible, active expression of the great missionary heart of Christ. The work of the church is outlined by various statements made by our Lord, such as Matthew 28:19–20, where he said to his disciples whom he was about to leave,

> Go therefore and make disciples of all nations, baptizing them in the name of the Father and of the Son and of the Holy Spirit, and teaching them to obey everything that I have commanded you. And remember, I am with you always, to the end of the age.

Here is how that Great Commission is recorded in Mark 16:15: "And he said to them, 'Go into all the world and proclaim the good news to the whole creation.'" It is the responsibility of the church and every Christian in it to go out with all the power of Christ's love and influence to win men and women, boys and girls everywhere to the Lord Jesus Christ.

The Church's Responsibilities

Other obligations are ours as Christians, affecting our duties and moral responsibilities to other human beings. We do not preach a "social gospel," but we certainly acknowledge and accept the social responsibilities that rest upon the church by its very character. We have a duty to aid the poor, clothe the naked, and visit the unfortunate. Jesus introduced the subject in the last third of Matthew 25. Certainly, the compassionate, caring heart of Christ should be manifested by his church. The Christlike nature of the church leads us to visit the widow, provide for the orphan, visit those who are sick and in prison. Paul even said, "If your enemies are hungry, feed them; if they are thirsty, give them something to drink" (Rom 12:20a).

As members of the New Testament church, we have a responsibility to honor civil authorities and obey the laws of the state. This is made explicit in Paul's letter to the church at Rome. Read carefully Romans 13, which begins with these words, "Let every person be subject to the governing authorities; for there is no authority except from God, and those authorities that exist have been instituted by God." What a strange thing for a Jew to say about Roman authority and rule! But Paul was a Christian as much as he was a Jew. The church is not a band of scofflaws who reject civil authority. Christians will obey the law at every point, except where laws of government run contrary to the revealed will of God. Then God's sovereignty will be respected above that of the state—and at any cost.

Church Organization

The organization of the early New Testament church was a very simple thing compared with what we see today. Christians served in the church where their God-given gifts made room for them. One became a prophet, not because a majority vote of the people so willed, but because God had bestowed upon that person the gift of prophecy. Teachers taught because God had called and qualified them for teaching. They did whatever they were divinely equipped to do. Others exercised certain other divinely bestowed gifts "to equip the saints for the work of ministry, for building up the body of Christ" (Eph 4:12). As these spiritual gifts were used, recognized, and honored, the church grew and prospered.[1]

There was no complex structuring of the church in the first century. Organization was kept at a minimum. When certain Greeks complained that widows in their congregation were being neglected in the daily ministrations, the twelve disciples met and decided that seven good men should be appointed to provide an equitable solution for the problem and then continue thus to minister in order that the hands and minds of the disciples might be freed for work of the ministry (Acts 6:1–7). When opposition caused the church in Jerusalem to be boycotted so that many of its members were impoverished and hungry, Paul simply gathered an offering from among the other churches to relieve this temporary need (Rom 15:25–27). The benevolent spirit of Christ, ruling in every Christian heart, was expected to prompt a proper care of widows and orphans (James 1:27). Every able-bodied man in the Christian fellowship was expected to work to earn his livelihood (2 Thess 3:10). Congregations prayed and then selected and sent out their own missionaries to evangelize the world (e.g., Acts 13:1–3).

True Christians respected the leadership abilities bestowed upon certain believers by God, as in the case of Paul. Paul possessed such integrity, wisdom, and other spiritual gifts that the saints followed his guidance and advice with constant profit. Through his sanctified judgment, pastors were supplied to particular congregations. He wrote to Titus, "I left you behind in Crete for this reason, so that you should put in order what remained to be done, and should appoint elders in every town, as I directed you" (1:5). A Jerusalem council of Christian leaders met voluntarily to pool their opinions with regard to certain doctrines and questions of conscience (Acts 15). Every believer was expected to be patient and

---

1. Editor's Note: Unlike some charismatic and neo-Pentecostal groups that teach that the Holy Spirit bestows both "serving" gifts (to edify and serve the church) and "signifying" gifts (to work miracles that signify the Spirit's presence), the Church of God understands that the Bible teaches all spiritual gifts are "serving" gifts: They equip individual Christians to serve the entire body of Christ (1 Cor 12:7–11). Their purpose is not to draw attention to the individual or to the church.

tolerant with anyone who happened to differ (1 Thess 5:14; 2 Tim 2:23–26). They seemed to need little by way of formal organization and bureaucratic machinery in those days.

The destiny of the church is bound up with our faithfulness to Christ. God's church was born in adversity, cradled in trouble, reared in the midst of opposition and conflict; yet it has overcome every foe—not by swords, chariots, and horsemen, but by a divine power inherent within it—by the power of almighty God. Where Christ is honored, loved, and obeyed, the church goes forward in conquering power. Where he is neglected, the church bogs down in the shallows and miseries of indecision, ineffectiveness, and un-fruitfulness. The chief law of the church is the law of love (Greek, *agape*), which Paul referred to as "the law of Christ" (Gal 6:2). The law of love prompts every action, motivates every program, and paves the way for every personal response to the divine call of God.

To love Christ, the great head of the church, is to obey him in all things. To love the lost for whom he died is to most highly honor him. To do all within our power to bring the lost to redemption is the clearest proof of our devotion to him.

So let the church do all within its power to be the church, the holy body of Christ, bending every effort to redeem humankind from destruction. At the same time, let the church live on a tiptoe of expectancy, yearning for the Master's soon return and ever praying, "Come, Lord Jesus!" (Rev 22:20).

Let us keep our lamps of watchfulness trimmed and burning, for at an hour of carelessness for millions of people, Christ will come for his holy bride, the church. In that high and holy hour, may he find his bride radiant, holy, pure, adorned with righteousness, eager and joyous at his coming!

Church of God Doctrine & History

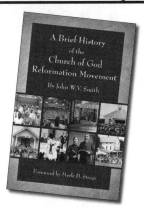

The Quest for Holiness and Unity
John W. V. Smith

The first official historian of the Church of God wrote this standard textbook on the rise and spread of the movement.

D6250

A Brief History of the Church of God Reformation Movement
John W. V. Smith

Now back in print, this digest history of the movement includes an update section and index.

1593171404

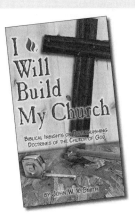

I Will Build My Church
John W. V. Smith

Dr. Smith traces how our teachings have developed and changed over the past 125 years.

D4320   Spanish: D4321

Heaven to Earth
(VHS or DVD)

This 1955 documentary explains how the Church of God emerged from the Holiness Revival.

VHS: D1005   DVD: 730817328157

Warner Press
In USA, call toll-free: 1-800-741-7721. Outside USA, call: 1-765-644-7721.

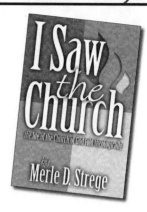
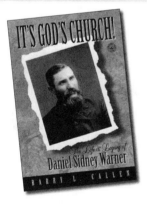
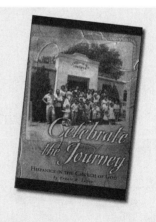

Church of God Doctrine & History

Logos Lesson Builder: Volume 1

More than 80 books by D. S. Warner and other first-generation Church of God ministers are contained on this CD-ROM.

D5000CD

Logos Lesson Builder: Volume 2

This collection of books by second-generation Church of God writers includes the work of F. G. Smith, C. E. Brown, and others.

Y5001CD

The Church of God as Revealed in Scripture
Arlo F. Newell

Dr. Newell guides us through New Testament teachings about the nature and ministry of the church.

D4775

Life in the Church
Arlo F. Newell

Reexamine the health of your congregation with this collection of editorials from *Vital Christianity*.

D5381

Warner Press

In USA, call toll-free: 1-800-741-7721. Outside USA, call: 1-765-644-7721.

Church of God Doctrine & History

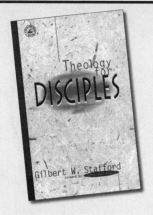

Theology for Disciples
Gilbert W. Stafford

Every layperson would profit from studying this up-to-date textbook of the movement's teachings.

9780871626745   **Study Guide:**
Thinking about Our Faith D5603

Christian Theology
Russell R. Byrum

First published in 1921, this classic text is still a valuable resource for studying Church of God doctrine.

D2450

O Church of God

Both children and adults love this seven-session multimedia study of the movement, which includes a DVD of *Heaven to Earth* and reproducible activity sheets.

K64100

Enriching Mind & Spirit
Barry L. Callen

Trace the history of Church of God higher education in North America. This attractive hardcover book has full-color photos.

Y9017

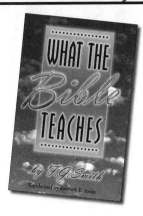

Basic Christian Theology
Albert F. Gray

The founder of Warner Pacific College wrote these doctrinal booklets for use as adult Sunday school electives.

Vol. 1: D7300   Vol. 2: D7301   Spanish (Vols. 1&2) Y1051

What the Bible Teaches
F. G. Smith

Long a doctrinal standard of the movement, this book is now available in a condensed edition by Kenneth E. Jones.

9780871621047   Spanish 9781593170448

Welcome to the Family
Oral & Laura Withrow

Introduce adults to the teachings and practices of the Church of God with this 13-week study.

D8775   Leader's Guide D8776

So You Want to Meet the Family
Jeff Hayes

This 13-week course helps teenagers explore what it means to be Christians actively involved in the Church of God.

D8310   Leader's Guide D8311

Warner Press

In USA, call toll-free: 1-800-741-7721. Outside USA, call: 1-765-644-7721.

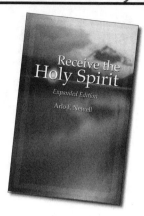

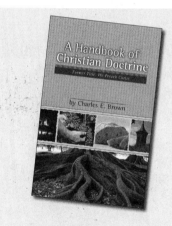